TOP **10**
BARCELONA

CONTENTS

BARCELONA

INTRODUCING

Barcelona skyline from Park Güell

WELCOME TO
BARCELONA

Sun-drenched, stylish and utterly captivating, Barcelona blends world-class art, historic treasures and cutting-edge design with effortless Mediterranean charm. Don't want to miss a thing? With Top 10 Barcelona, you'll enjoy the very best the city has to offer.

This is a city where the past comes alive, 2,000 years of history whispering from Roman walls and medieval palaces. Nowhere exemplifies this better than the Gothic Quarter, a labyrinth of historic stone lanes and squares overlooked by spitting gargoyles and an epic 12-century cathedral. Leap forward in time as you amble down tree-lined La Rambla, marvelling at Modernista mansions by architects who made the city their playground at the turn of the 20th century. Spot buildings resembling dragons (Casa Batlló) or ice-cream (La Pedrera), and wander through the

Buzzing local life in Barcelona

ity's favourite park, the Park Güell, all
esigned by Antoni Gaudí. His most
conic creation, the Sagrada Família,
s visible from almost everywhere, the
pires reaching higher each day as
t finally approaches completion. It's
ot just the architects who have been
reaking ground here: seek out the
Museu Nacional d'Art de Catalunya or
he eponymous museums dedicated
o the works of Picasso and Miro to
ee how the city has inspired artists
or centuries and continues to do so.

This isn't the Spain of flamenco
and orange trees: this is Barcelona,
proud capital of Catalunya, with its
own language and traditions. Wander
hrough the city's patchwork neigh-
ourhoods and you'll see that this

independent spirit courses through
all aspects of life. It's in the incredible
local festivals, where locals dress
as demons and dodge fire-spitting
dragons. It's in the centuries-old local
dishes that remain quintessentially
Catalan no matter how many times
they're reinvented. And it's in the
unrivalled passions found at the
Camp Nou football stadium, where
the city congregates to watch world-
famous FC Barcelona.

So, where to start? With Top 10
Barcelona, of course. This pocket-
sized guide gets to the heart of the
city with simple lists of ten, expert
local knowledge and comprehensive
maps, helping you turn an ordinary
trip into an extraordinary one.

THE STORY OF
BARCELONA

Barcelona's story, from Roman backwater to international hotspot, is a wild one. The city's fortunes, often tied to the wider Catalonian region, have seen the glory days of its medieval trading empire and crushing defeat in the terrible siege of 1714 – and yet it's always come back better than before. Here's the story of how it came to be.

Barcelona Begins

Though evidence of settlements dates back to 5000 BCE, it wasn't until around 1000 BCE that this fertile region, then known as Barkeno, was more permanently settled by the Laietani, an Iberian people. The city began to take shape under the Romans, who established a settlement here during their inexorable conquest of the entire Iberian peninsula (modern Spain and Portugal) in around 218 BCE. Barcelona (now known as Barcino) remained in the shadow of the provincial capital of Tarraco (modern Tarragona) but grew quietly prosperous on agriculture and wine, which was exported all over the empire. By the end of the 2nd century CE, the population had grown to 5,000 and Barcelona was thriving. As the Roman empire began to disintegrate, however, several Germanic tribes took advantage of th cracks to thrust south into modern-d Spain, conquering swathes of territor

Thieving Visigoths and Conquering Caliphate

Few of the Germanic tribes lingered i Barcelona: most plundered and left, until the arrival of the Visigoths in the early 5th century. The Visigothic chief Ataulf (c 370–415) made the affluent and well-fortified port city his capital constructing the Visigothic basilica (remnants of which are still visible beneath the Palau Reial, *p82*) and ushering in a brief era of peace. As the Visigothic Kingdom established its ho across former Roman Hispania, the capital shifted to Toledo and Barcelor slipped into decline. In 711, the armie of the Umayyad Caliphate crossed fror

Roman mosaic depicting the sacrifice of Iphigenia

The Umayyad Caliphate conquering the Spanish peninsula in 711

North Africa and rapidly took control of much of Hispania. They conquered Tarraco in 717, brutally laying the city to waste, and Barcelona surrendered peacefully in order to avoid the same fate. The result was nearly a century of Muslim rule that saw the city's cathedral converted into a mosque.

The Birth of Catalunya

Determined to restore Christianity and expand their territories beyond France, the Franks pushed back against the advance of the Muslim armies and, after a lengthy siege in 801, Louis the Pious, son of Charlemagne, captured Barcelona. The city initially came under the rule of local lords before the newly appointed Count of Barcelona took control of the city and wider Catalan region on behalf of the Carolingian empire. In 878 the first such count, Wilfred the Hairy (Guifré el Pelós), brought together several Catalan counties, including Barcelona, and established a hereditary dynasty that would last 500 years. In the centuries that followed, Barcelona broke away from Frankish control and grew rich through trading and the dynastic union in 1137 between Catalonia and Aragon. It became a leading European city known for dazzling Romanesque and Gothic art and architecture, major trading routes across the Mediterranean and even a burgeoning empire that briefly stretched as far as Athens.

Moments in History

550 BCE
Greeks establish a trading settlement at Empúries.

878 CE
The Count of Barcelona is established by the Franks and given control of an area of the Spanish Marches that includes Barcelona.

1348-75
Five outbreaks of the Black Death in Barcelona decimates the population.

1714
Barcelona falls to the Bourbon armies after a brutal 13-month-long siege, during which 7,000 locals were killed and 40,000 cannon shots were fired.

1848
The first railway line in Spain opens, linking Barcelona with Mataró, key ports for the cotton industry.

1936

A military uprising is thwarted by the Catalan government and trade union groups, contributing to the outbreak of the Spanish Civil War.

1977

The exiled president of Catalunya, Josep Tarradellas, returns to Barcelona and the Catalan Government (*Generalitat*) is restored.

1992

The Summer Olympic Games are held in Barcelona and become one of the most successful on record, both financially and culturally.

2017

A Catalan independence referendum is held in defiance of the Spanish government, who deem it illegal, and independence is briefly declared.

2022

Barcelona becomes the first city to win the Biosphere Platinum Certificate in recognition of their sustainable tourism policies.

Boom turns to Bust

Despite the prosperity, there were signs that it couldn't last. The 14th century had seen plague and famine ravage the city, while Jewish pogroms had devastated the local population. When much of Spain was united through marriage in 1469, power began to transfer from Barcelona to Madrid, with the Castilian rulers shutting Barcelona out of trade with the new empire in the Americans. Growing tensions led the Catalan region to fight against the Spanish crown during both the Thirty Years' War and the War of Spanish Succession. During the latter, Barcelona fell to the Bourbon armies under Philip V after resisting the merciless siege for almost 14 months – the date (11 September 1714) is still commemorated as Catalan National Day. The new Bourbon rulers banned the Catalan language, abolished the region's political institutions and built a huge fortress to watch over Barcelona.

Catalan Renaissance and Dictatorship

Despite such subjugation, Barcelona rebounded and expanded through the 19th-century industrial revolution, constructing Spain's first railway line

Signing The Treaty of the Pyrenees, ending the Franco-Spanish war

General Franco making a speech to the residents of Tarragona

(linking Barcelona and Mataró) and becoming one of the world's largest centres of cotton production. With the new-found affluence came a renewed pride in Catalan language and culture, known as the *Renaixença*. This was expressed in art, literature and the Modernisme architecture, a style developed by Antoni Gaudí and Lluís Domènech i Montaner that captured the essence of Catalan identity.

In 1887, the first home rule party, the Lliga de Catalunya, was founded, and by the early 20th century there were increasingly forceful calls for regional autonomy from Spain. This momentum peaked in 1931, when Catalan president Francesc Macià declared the Republic of Catalunya, but this independence was soon quashed by the bloody Spanish Civil War. Barcelona was the centre of Republican forces and was heavily bombed by the Nationalists under General Franco. After the Nationalist victory in 1939, Catalan autonomy was stripped away and its language and traditions severely repressed.

Barcelona Today

After Franco's death in 1975, constitutional democracy was restored with the establishment of 17 autonomous regions, including Catalunya, and the reinstalling of the regional government *(Generalitat)*. The newly revitalized city was chosen to host the 1992 Olympics, embarking on a huge renovation plan that transformed the skyline and put Barcelona well and truly on the tourist map. However, tensions over independence have continued to simmer, reaching boiling points during the economic crises of the early 21st century. A 2017 independence referendum was declared illegal by the Spanish government. Nonetheless, Barcelona remains one of the most popular destinations in Europe thanks to its combination of art, history and culture of inclusivity, while also becoming a world-leading smart city, recognized for its innovative policies to address global challenges such as climate change.

Pro-independence flags on Catalonia's National Day

TOP 10
EXPERIENCES

Planning the perfect trip to Barcelona? Whether you're visiting for the first time or making a return trip, there are some things you simply shouldn't miss out on. To make the most of your time – and to enjoy the very best this glorious Mediterranean city has to offer – be sure to add these experiences to your list.

1 Escape to the beach
Thanks to Barcelona's magnificent Mediterranean setting, the city has more than 4 km (2 miles) of gorgeous sandy beaches, perfect for soaking up the sun while relaxing, a refreshing dip in the sea or for trying an exciting new activity such as windsurfing or beach volleyball.

2 Attend a festa major
Barcelona hosts fantastic neighbourhood festivals (*festes* in Catalan) that feature folkloric traditions, from dancing *gegants* (giants) to the anarchic *correfocs* (fire-running), in which fire-spitting dragons career through the streets. There's also often live music, outdoor bars and big street parties.

3 Climb the towers of the Sagrada Família
The interior of Antoni Gaudí's Sagrada Família is spellbinding, but it's the views from the towers that will take your breath away. Step out of the lift to find the city spread out below your feet, and come back down to earth via a spiral staircase.

4 Explore Roman history
Barcelona's medieval heart contains a palimpsest of Roman Barcino, with Roman walls, baths and temple columns incorporated into Gothic buildings. Walk in the footsteps of the Romans at MUHBA (Museum of the History of Barcelona), which holds the largest Roman excavation outside Rome.

5 Hop on a ride at Tibidabo

Tibidabo, Barcelona's tallest mountain at 517 m (1,695 ft), is home to a panoramic amusement park with dizzying views over the entire city. Ride traditional attractions including a beautifully preserved red plane from 1917 and a colourful Ferris wheel.

6 Catch a football match

See the city's legendary football team, FC Barcelona, live at the Olympic Stadium (their Camp Nou stadium is being remodelled and should be ready for the 2025/26 season) or in city bars packed with hordes of passionate local fans.

7 Visit the city's art museums

Barcelona is home to an excellent array of museums showcasing more than a millennia of Catalan art, from the Romanesque frescoes at MNAC to the works of 20th-century giants Pablo Picasso, Joan Miró and Antoni Tàpies.

8 Relax in green spaces

The city's parks provide a peaceful respite from the tightly packed urban sprawl of Barcelona. The Parc de la Ciutadella is a gorgeous green oasis while the lovely parks and gardens on Montjuïc are perfect for a picnic among the flowers, with fantastic city views.

9 Taste Mediterranean paella

Paella – originally from Valencia – is just one of the delectable rice dishes found along Spain's Mediterranean coast, and a long, languid lunch, particularly at a beachfront restaurant, will provide an unforgettable dining experience.

10 Sip on local vermouth

"La hora del vermut" ("the vermouth hour") is a beloved local tradition: friends and family gather for a pre-lunch drink featuring vermouth, a fortified wine made all over southern Europe including in Catalonia, and some simple tapas such as olives or anchovies.

ITINERARIES

Seeking out the best paella, strolling along La Rambla, ogling the unique works of Gaudí: there's a lot to see and do in Barcelona. With places to eat, drink or simply take in the view, these itineraries offer ways to spend 2 days and 4 days in the city.

2 DAYS

Eccentric exterior of Casa Batlló, designed by Antoni Gaudí

Day 1

Morning
Begin your visit in the Plaça de Sant Jaume (p81), an expansive square that has been home to the city's rulers since the middle ages. Stand at its centre to really appreciate the Gothic architectural masterpieces such as the Palau de la Generalitat, the seat of the Catalonian government (p81), and the Ajuntament, City Hall. From the square, plunge into the atmospheric streets of El Call (p82), the old Jewish Quarter, to wander the narrow lanes until you reach the Sinagoga Major de Barcelona (sinagoga-mayor.com), one of the oldest synagogues in Europe. Make a pitstop at

> **EAT**
> Inside Santa Caterina market, you'll find a couple of great counter bars: the Bar Joan, famous for its great value set lunches (it always serves paella on Thursdays) and the Bar L'Univers, with tasty tapas, including delicious seafood.

Salterio (p88) for its amazing array of teas, before emerging out of the narrow lanes onto the pretty Plaça Felip Neri (p84). From here it's just a stone's throw to Barcelona's splendid cathedral (p28), designed in a Catalonian Gothic style and dating back to 1298.

Afternoon
Head east across the Via Laietana until you spot the undulating, multicoloured roof of the Santa Caterina market, where you can sit down for lunch at Cuines Santa Caterina (grupotragaluz.com) amid the heaped produce stalls. Walk off your lunch with a wander up the elegant Passeig de Gràcia to marvel at the city's finest Modernista buildings, stopping to explore the rooms of the fairy-tale Casa Batlló (p50), perhaps Antoni Gaudí's greatest masterpiece. Continue on to admire the rippling façade of La Pedrera (p34), another extraordinary building sprung from the unbounded imagination of Gaudí. Finish up today with a divine dinner at Windsor (p117), one of the city's finest restaurants for Catalan cuisine.

Barcelona Cathedral lit up on a clear evening

Day 2

Morning

Start today with a visit to the Gaudí designed Park Güell (p32): an early start is recommended to beat the crowds, as is pre-booking tickets. Take time to explore the many brilliant parts of the park and then wander through the elegant boulevards of the Gràcia neighbourhood. Here you can take a break on the beautiful Plaça de la Virreina – La Cafetera (p123) is great for coffee or a *vermut* (vermouth) – before popping into the boutiques along Carrer Verdi, including Picnic and Nana Banana (p122). Linger over a well-deserved tapas lunch on the sunny terrace at Marcelino *(Plaça del Sol 2)* on another of Gràcia's beautiful squares, the Plaça del Sol (p53).

Afternoon

A 20-minute walk or a quick hop on the metro (line 5 from Diagonal to Sagrada Família) brings you to the Gothic and Art Nouveau marvel the Sagrada Família *(p22)*, where you can spend the afternoon admiring Gaudí's genius in his largest and most celebrated creation. Be sure to take the lift up the towers for phenomenal views over the city. Then it's time to jump on the metro (taking line 5 from Sagrada Familia to Verdaguer, then line 4 to Barceloneta) to head down to the beach for an *aperitiu* (appetizer) before a wonderful dinner with sea views at Barraca *(p109)*.

SHOP

Gràcia is famous for its fabulous independent fashion boutiques, particularly along Carrer Verdi and Carrer Bonavista. If you're looking for gourmet treats, check out the specialist shops around the Mercat de la Llibertat.

Map labels:

0 metres 800
0 yards 800

② Park Güell

La Cafetera
Plaça de la Virreina
Carrer Verdi
Plaça del Sol
Marcelino

GRÀCIA

Windsor

Diagonal
Verdaguer
METRO LINE 5
Sagrada Família
Sagrada Família

La Pedrera

Casa Batlló

EIXAMPLE

Passeig de Gràcia

METRO LINE 4

BARRI GÒTIC

Santa Caterina Market

see inset below

Plaça Felip Neri
Sinagoga Major
Salterio
Catedral
① Plaça de Sant Jaume

Barceloneta

Barraca

0 metres 200
0 yards 200

to Velódromo →

0 metres 400
0 yards 400

Velódromo · Day 4

0 km 1
0 miles 1

Sant Antoni
Market
3

MONTJUÏC

Fundació
Joan Miró

see main map

POBLEN

Day 2

Er

Miramar
Station

CABLE CAR

BARCELONETA

· Torre d'Alta Mar

El Gallito

Casa
Batlló

Passeig de ·
Gràcia

Museu d'Art
Contemporani
de Barcelona
(MACBA)
4

Carrer
· Tallers

EL RAVAL

Caravelle

La Rambla

Clemen's ·

Plaça de
Catalunya

Palau de la
Música Catalana

· Café L'Antiquari

· La Boqueria

Barcelona Cathedral
1

Museu d'Història
de Barcelona

BARRI
GÒTIC

Santa Maria
del Mar

2 Picasso
Museum

Casa
Delfí

· Parc de la
Ciutadella

to F
Poble

4 DAYS

Day 1

Start your four-day sojourn by soaking up Barcelona's history in the enchanting Gothic Quarter. At Museu d'Història de Barcelona (MUHBA, *p82*) discover the largest subterranean Roman ruins in Europe, the throne room where Christopher Columbus met Spanish monarchs and a jewel-box Gothic church. More history can be found next door at Barcelona's medieval cathedral

(*p28*) with its splendid Gothic interior and graceful cloister. Afterwards, stroll along La Rambla (*p26*) to La Boqueria, a produce market packed with around 330 stalls, for lunch at Clemen's. Once refuelled, head to the Palau de la Músic Catalana (*p40*), for a tour of this magni ficent Modernista music hall with its stunning stained-glass skylight. Follow that with dinner overlooking a mediev square at Café L'Antiquari (*p89*).

Day 2

Today begins by exploring some of the 5,000 works at the excellent Picasso Museum (*p38*), housed across five Gothi palaces. Spend much of the morning here before ambling over to the breath taking Gothic church of Santa Maria de Mar, often referred to as "the cathedra

> **VIEW**
> Take the lift to Barcelona Cathedral's rooftop to admire city-wide views in the company of the cathedral gargoyles – there are over 160 of them, including an elephant and a unicorn.

The steel-framed Mercat de Sant Antoni

by the sea" *(p82)*. Explore its striking, unadorned interior and soak up the fabulous views from the rooftop. After a delicious lunch at Casa Delfín *(p89)*, enjoy a leisurely stroll through the Parc de la Ciutadella *(p106)*, the largest green space in the city centre. Hire a rowboat for a punt around the lake, with ducks, swans and herons for company, before hitting the trendy streets of Poblenou, where you can tuck into creative tapas at El 58 *(Rambla de Poblenou 58)*.

Day 3

Grab a breakfast bite at the gorgeously restored Sant Antoni Market *(p70)*, where

The majestic 14th-century Santa Maria del Mar church

stalls are heaped with fresh, local produce, before heading up to the leafy Montjuïc. Spend the rest of the morning admiring the superb artworks at the Fundació Joan Miró *(p36)*, where you can also enjoy stunning city-wide views from the terrace and enjoy a relaxed lunch at the museum café. Once full, stroll down to the Miramar cable car station to hop on one of the little red cable cars that swing across the port to Barceloneta. Here you can unwind on the beach and take a dip in the sea, before strolling down the seafront to El Gallito *(p109)* to savour seafood specialities as you watch dusk fall over the Mediterranean.

Day 4

Spend a morning with the modern art at Museu d'Art Contemporani de Barcelona (MACBA, *p36*), set in a dazzling white building in the heart of the El Raval neighbourhood. After a coffee break at the museum café, it's time to shop. Head up to Carrer Tallers for some excellent vintage fashion shops *(p92)*, before a light lunch at Caravelle *(p97)*. Then cross the bustling Plaça de Catalunya to reach the Passeig de Gràcia; this elegant avenue is where you'll find high street chains mixed with global fashion labels. It's also where the best examples of Modernista mansions are, including the colourful Casa Batlló *(p50)*, which is the perfect final stop on your visit. Finish with a relaxed dinner and drinks at the always buzzy Velodrómo *(p116)*.

TOP 10 HIGHLIGHTS

Casa Mila

EXPLORE THE
HIGHLIGHTS

There are some sights in Barcelona you simply shouldn't miss, and it's these attractions that make the Top 10. Discover what makes each one a must-see on the following pages.

LES CORTS

CARRER DEL MIG DE SANTS

RONDA

RONDA DE SANT PAU

AVINGUDA DEL PARAL·LEL

❹

MONTJUÏC

❼

Parc de Montjuïc

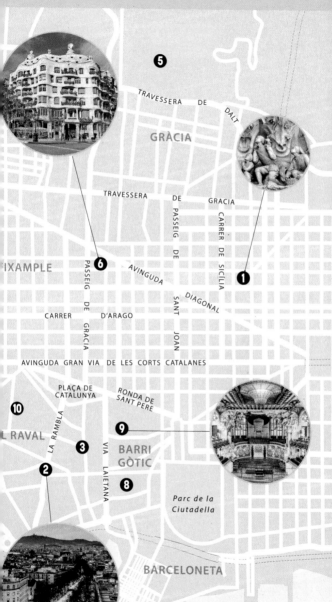

TRAVESSERA   DE   DALT

GRÀCIA

❺

TRAVESSERA   DE   GRACIA

PASSEIG   DE

CARRER   DE   SICÍLIA

IXAMPLE

PASSEIG   DE   GRACIA

AVINGUDA   DIAGONAL

❻

SANT   JOAN

CARRER   D'ARAGO

❶

AVINGUDA   GRAN   VIA   DE   LES   CORTS   CATALANES

PLAÇA DE
CATALUNYA

RONDA DE
SANT PERE

❿

L RAVAL

LA RAMBLA

❾

❸

VIA   LAIETANA

**BARRI
GÒTIC**

❷

❽

*Parc de la
Ciutadella*

BARCELONETA

| 0 meters | | 500 |
| 0 yards | | 500 |

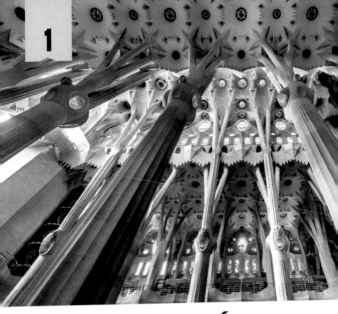

SAGRADA FAMÍLIA

📍 G2 🏠 Entrances: C/Marina (for groups only) and C/Sardenya ⏰ 9am–6pm daily (Mar & Oct: to 7pm; Apr–Sep: to 8pm) 🌐 sagradafamilia.org 📷📍

Antoni Gaudí's Sagrada Família is a *tour de force* of the imagination. It offers visitors the unique chance to watch a wonder of the world in the making. Over the last 90 years, sculptors and architects have continued to build Gaudí's dream and the remarkable 175-m- (570-ft-) high central tower is slated for completion in 2026, Gaudí's 100th death anniversary.

The Sagrada Família, reflected in water

1 Spiral Staircases

These helicoidal stone stairways, which wind up the bell towers, look like snail shells.

2 Nave

The immense central body of the church, now complete, is made up of leaning, tree-like columns with beautiful branches that are inspired by a banana tree spreading out across the ceiling. The overall effect is that of a mesmerizing stone forest.

TOP TIP

The light on the Nativity Façade before 8am is ideal for taking photos.

3 Hanging Model

This contraption is testimony to Gaudí's ingenuity. He made the 3D device – using chains and tiny weighted sacks of lead pellets – as a model for the arches and vaulted ceilings of the Colonia Güell crypt.

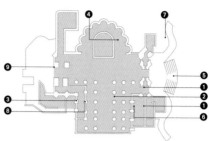

Sagrada Família Floorplan

the church's soaring nave and spectacular ceiling

4 Apse
Adorned with serpents, four large snails and lizards, this was the first section to be completed by Gaudí. Here, the stained glass graduates in tones beautifully.

5 Nativity Façade
Gaudí's love of nature is visible in this elegant façade, the oldest façade in the building. Up to 100 plant and animal species

are sculpted in stone, and the two main columns are supported by turtles.

6 Spires
Gaudí's plan originally detailed a total of 18 spires. For a closer look at the mosaic tiling and gargoyles on the existing spires, take the lift up inside the bell tower. The views are equally spectacular.

7 Rosario's Claustro
In the only cloister to be finished by Gaudí, the imagery is thought to be inspired by the anarchist riots that began in 1909. The Devil's temptation of man is depicted by the sculpture of a serpent wound around a rebel.

8 Crypt Museum
Gaudí now lies in the crypt, and his tomb is visible from the museum. Using audio-visual exhibits, the museum provides a lot of information about the construction of the church. The highlight is the maquette workshop, producing scale models for the ongoing work.

9 Passion Façade
Created between 1954 and 2002, this Josep Subirachs façade represents the sacrifice and pain of Jesus. The difference between the Gothic feel of Subirachs' style and the intricacy of Gaudí's work has been controversial.

10 Unfinished Business
The church buzzes with activity even today. Sculptors dangle from spires, stonemasons carve huge slabs of stone, and cranes and scaffolding litter the site. Watching the construction in progress reveals the monumental scale of this epic project.

Intricately carved sculptures on the Nativity Façade

Key Sagrada Família Dates

1. 1882
The first stone of the Sagrada Família is officially laid, with architect Francesc del Villar heading the project. Villar soon resigns after disagreements with the church's religious founders.

2. 1883
The young, up-and-coming Antoni Gaudí is commissioned as the principal architect. He goes on to devote the next 40 years of his life to the project: by the end he even lives on the premises.

3. 1889
The church crypt is completed, ringed by a series of chapels, one of which is later to house Gaudí's tomb.

4. 1904
The final touches are made to the Nativity Façade, which depicts Jesus, Mary and Joseph amid a chorus of angels.

5. 1925
The first of the 18 planned bell towers, measuring 100 m (330 ft) in height, is finished.

One of Subirachs' striking sculptures on the Passion Façade

6. 1926
On 10 June, Gaudí is killed by a tram while crossing the street near his beloved church.

7. 1936
The military uprising and the Spanish Civil War brings construction of the Sagrada Família to a halt for some 20 years. During this period, Gaudí's studio and the crypt in the Sagrada Família are burned by revolutionaries, who despise the Catholic church for siding with the nationalists.

8. 1987–1990
Sculptor and painter Josep Maria Subirachs (b 1927) takes to living in the church just as his famous predecessor did. Subirachs completes the statuary of the Passion Façade. His angular sculptures draw both criticism and praise.

9. 2000
On 31 December, the nave is at long last declared complete.

10. 2010–2023
The central nave of the church has been completed, and in 2010 Pope Benedict XVI consecrated it as a basilica. The Lion of Judah, among other things, was added to the Passion Façade in 2018, marking its completion. The tower of the Virgin Mary was completed in 2021, followed by the four towers dedicated to the Evangelists in 2022–23.

Sagrada Família's crypt, Gaudí's final resting place

ANTONI GAUDÍ

A flag bearer for the Modernista movement of the late 19th century, Antoni Gaudí is Barcelona's most famous architect and has become a globally celebrated figure. A strong Catalan nationalist and a devout Catholic, he led an almost monastic life, consumed by his architectural vision and living in virtual poverty. In 2003, the Vatican opened the beatification process for Gaudí, which is the first step towards declaring his sainthood. Gaudí's extraordinary legacy dominates the architectural map of Barcelona. His name itself comes from the Catalan verb *gaudir*, meaning "to enjoy", and an enormous sense of exuberance and playfulness pervades his work. As was characteristic of Modernisme, nature prevails, not only in the decorative motifs, but also in the very structure of Gaudí's buildings. His highly innovative style is also characterized by intricate wrought-iron gates and balconies and *trencadís* tiling.

Antoni Gaudí, one of the best known Catalan architects and *(right)* his greatest masterpiece, the magnificent and colourful Casa Batlló

LA RAMBLA

One of the city's best-loved sights, the historic La Rambla avenue splits the Old Town in half as it stretches from Plaça de Catalunya to Port Vell. Teeming with locals, tourists and performance artists, this street has long been a lively hub of exuberant activity. There may be no better place in the country to indulge in the Spanish ritual of the *paseo* (stroll). An ambitious renovation plan, slated for completion in 2027, is making La Rambla greener and more pedestrian-friendly.

1 Gran Teatre del Liceu

L4 ⌂ La Rambla 51–59 W liceu barcelona.cat

The city's grand opera house, founded in 1847, brought Catalan opera stars such as Montserrat Caballé to the world. Twice gutted by fire, the building has now been fully restored.

2 Mercat de la Boqueria

L3 ⌂ La Rambla 91 ⌚ 8am–8:30pm Mon–Sat W boqueria. barcelona

A cacophonous shrine to food, this cavernous market has it all, from stacks of fruit to suckling pigs and fresh lobsters.

3 Flower Stalls

La Rambla is bursting with life and things to distract the eye, but the true Rambla stalwarts are the flower stalls flanking the pedestrian walkway, many run by the same families for decades.

4 Arts Santa Mònica

L5 ⌂ La Rambla 7 ⌚ 11am–8:30pm Tue–Sun W artssanta monica.gencat.cat

Once the haunt of rosary beads and prayers, this former 17th-century monastery was reborn in the 1980s as a contemporary art centre, thanks to government funding. This "Centre de la Creativitat" lays special emphasis on encouraging creativity in Catalunya and promoting home-grown talent. Exhibitions here showcase a range of artworks by a mix of both local and international artists, from large-scale video installations to photography.

Enjoying a meal at the Mercat de la Boqueria

The bustling La Rambla, Barcelona's most famous promenade

5 Monument a Colom

Pointing resolutely out to sea, this 1888 bronze statue *(p106)* of Christopher Columbus marks his return to Spain after his infamous journey to the Americas. An elevator whisks visitors to the top of the column for stunning views over the city.

6 Font de Canaletes

Ensure that you come back to the city by supping water from this 19th-century fountain. According to local legend, those who drink from it "will fall in love with Barcelona and always return to it".

7 Palau de la Virreina

📍 L3 🏠 La Rambla 99
🕐 11am–8pm Tue–Sun
🌐 ajuntament.barcelona.cat/lavirreina

This Neo-Classical palace was built by the viceroy of Peru in 1778. Today, the Palace of the Viceroy's Wife is home to the Centre de la Imatge, and hosts art exhibitions and cultural events.

8 Miró Mosaic

On the walkway on La Rambla is a colourful floor mosaic by Catalan artist Joan Miró. Symbolizing the cosmos, it incorporates his signature abstract shapes and primary colours.

9 Església de Betlem

📍 L2 🏠 C/Xuclà 2
🕐 8:30am–1:30pm & 6–9pm daily
🌐 mdbetlem.com

From a time when the Catholic Church in Spain was rolling in pesetas (and power), this hulking 17th-century church is a seminal reminder of a time when La Rambla was more religious than risqué.

10 Bruno Quadras Building

Once an umbrella factory, this remarkable late 19th-century building is decorated with Chinese-inspired motifs. Its exterior is festooned with umbrellas and a Chinese dragon statue.

A Chinese dragon statue on the Bruno Quadras' façade

BARCELONA CATHEDRAL

📍 M3 📍 Pl de la Seu 🕐 9:30am–6:30pm Mon–Fri, 9:30am–5:15pm Sat, 2–5pm Sun 🌐 catedralbcn.org 📍

From its Gothic cloister and Baroque chapels to its 19th-century façade, Barcelona's Seu, or cathedral, is an amalgam of architectural styles. While it dates from 1298, records show that a Christian baptistry was established here in the 6th century, later replaced by a Romanesque basilica in the 11th century, which gave way to the current cathedral.

1 Casa de l'Ardiaca
📍 M3 📍 C/Santa Llúcia 1 🕐 10am–2pm & 3–7:30pm Mon–Fri, by appointment Originally built in the 12th century, the Archdeacon's House is located near what was once the Bishop's Gate in the city's Roman walls. It now includes a leafy patio with a fountain.

2 Choir Stalls
The lavish choir stalls (1340), crowned with wooden spires, are decorated with colourful coats of arms by artist Joan de Borgonya.

3 Cloister
Graced with a fountain, palm trees and roaming geese, the cloister dates back

> **TOP TIP**
>
> See the Sardana folk dance performed in Plaça de la Seu, next to the cathedral.

Vaulted ceilings soar above the cloisters

plendid interior of
arcelona Cathedral

o the 14th century.
he mossy fountain
 presided over by
 small iron statue
f Sant Jordi, or
t George (p47).

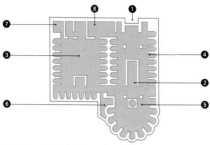

Barcelona Cathedral Floorplan

4 Nave and Organ

he immense nave
s supported by slender
olumns and features
 raised high altar.
he 16th-century
rgan looming over
he interior fills the
pace with music
during services.

5 Crypt of Santa Eulàlia

n the centre of the
rypt lies the graceful
327 alabaster sarco-
hagus of Santa Eulàlia,
arcelona's first patron
aint. Reliefs depict
er martyrdom.

6 Roof Terrace

Access the roof
terrace via a lift to
enjoy close-up views
of the magnificent
spire, belltowers and
gargoyles, as well
as over the medieval
rooftops of the old city.

7 Capella de Santa Llúcia

This lovely Romanesque
chapel is dedicated
to Santa Llúcia, the
patron saint of eyes
and vision. On her saint's
day (13 December),
the blind come to
pray at her chapel.

8 Capella del Santíssim i Crist de Lepant

This 15th-century chapel
features the Crist de
Lepant, which, legend has
it, guided the Christian
fleet in the 16th-century
Battle of Lepanto against
the Ottoman Turks.

9 Pia Almoina and Museu Diocesà

◉ N3 ◉ Av de la
Catedral 4 ◉ 10am–
8pm daily (from
11am Tue) ◉
The 11th-century Pia
Almoina, once a rest
house for pilgrims
and the poor, houses
the Museu Diocesà,
which contains some
of the cathedral's
finest paintings,
sculptures, fabrics
and numismatics.

10 Main Façade

The 19th-century
façade has the grand
entrance, flanked by
twin towers, Modernista
stained-glass windows
and 100 carved angels.
The restoration here
took eight years and
was completed in 2011.

The cathedral's Neo-Gothic façade and towers

MUSEU NACIONAL D'ART DE CATALUNYA

B4 · Palau Nacional, Parc de Montjuïc · 10am–6pm Tue–Sat (May–Sep: to 8pm), 10am–3pm Sun · museunacional.cat

Holding one of the most important medieval art collections in the world, the Museu Nacional d'Art de Catalunya (MNAC) is housed in the majestic Palau Nacional, built in 1929. A highlight is the Romanesque art section, which consists of the painted interiors of Pyrenean churches dating from the 11th and 12th centuries.

1 The Madonna of the Councillors

Commissioned by the city council in 1443, this work by Lluís Dalmau is rich in political symbolism, with the head councillors, saints and martyrs kneeling before an enthroned Virgin.

2 Murals: Santa Maria de Taüll

The well-preserved interior of Santa Maria de Taüll (c 1123) gives an idea of how colourful the Romanesque churches must have been. There are scenes from Jesus's early life, with John the Baptist and the Wise Men.

3 Cambó Bequest

Catalan politician Francesc Cambó (1876–1974) left his huge art collection to Catalonia; two large galleries contain works from the 16th to early 19th centuries, including Tiepolo's 1756 *The Minuet*.

4 Thyssen-Bornemisza Collection

The museum has a small but fine selection from Baron Thyssen-Bornemisza's extensive collection. Among the paintings are Fra Angelico's *Madonna of Humility* (1433–5) and a charmingly domestic *Madonna and Child* (c 1618) by Peter Paul Rubens.

5 Frescoes: Sant Climent de Taüll

The interior of Sant Climent de Taüll is a melange of French,

> **GALLERY GUIDE**
> The Cambó Bequest, with Zurbarán's and Goya's works, and the Thyssen-Bornemisza Collection, are on the ground floor, as are the Romanesque worhs. On the first floor are the modern art galleries and the photography and numismatics collections.

Left Madonna and Child by Rubens
Above Exhibits at the Museu Nacional
d'Art de Catalunya

yzantine and Italian
fluences. The apse is
ominated by *Christ in
ajesty* and the symbols
the four Evangelists
nd the Virgin, with the
ostles beneath.

**Ramon Casas
and Pere Romeu
n a Tandem**
his painting depicts
e painter Casas and his
iend Romeu, with whom
e began the Barri Gòtic
vern Els Quatre Gats.

**Woman
with Hat
nd Fur Collar**
casso's extraordinary
epiction of his lover
aria-Thérèse Walter
ows him moving
eyond Cubism and
urrealism into a new
ersonal language, soon
be known simply as
e "Picasso style".

**Crucifix of
Batlló Majesty**
his mid-12th century
ooden carving is a
epiction of Christ on

scading waterfalls below
e striking Palau Nacional

the cross with open
eyes and no signs of
suffering, as he has
defeated death.

**9 Confidant from
the Batlló House**
Among the fine
Modernista furnish-
ings are some exquisite
pieces by Antoni Gaudí,
including an undulating
wooden chair designed to
encourage confidences
between friends.

10 Numismatics
This public
collection of currency
dates back to the 6th
century BCE and features
a vast array of historical
items. On display here
are medals, early paper
money, 15th-century
Italian bills and coins,
including examples from
the Greek colony of
Empúries, which had
its own mint from the
5th century BCE.

Museu Nacional d'Art de Catalunya Floorplan

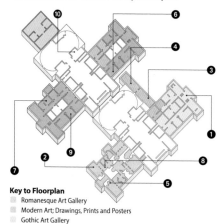

Key to Floorplan
- Romanesque Art Gallery
- Modern Art; Drawings, Prints and Posters
- Gothic Art Gallery
- Renaissance and Baroque Art
- Library

PARK GÜELL

📍 C1 🏠 C/d'Olot s/n ⏰ Hours vary, chech website 🌐 parkguell.barcelona ↗

Built between 1900 and 1914, Park Güell was conceived as an English-style garden city by Gaudí's patron, Eusebi Güell, who envisaged villas gardens and public spaces. However, the project failed. The space was sold to the city and, in 1926, reopened as a public park where Gaudí had let his imagination run riot on the pavilions, stairways, main square and marketplace, much of which is now in the ticketed Monumental Area.

The park's bench, made with pieces of tiles

1 Sala Hipòstila
The park's marketplace was the product of Josep Jujol, one of Gaudí's most gifted collaborators. Responsible for decorating the 84 columns here, he crafted vivid ceiling mosaics from shards of broken tiles.

2 Tiled Bench
An enormous bench, which functions as a balustrade, ripples around the edge of Plaça de la Natura. Artists ranging from Miró to Dalí were inspired by its abstract designs created from colourful broken tiles.

3 Jardins d'Àustria
These beautifully manicured gardens are modern, laid out in the 1970s on what was originally destined to be a plot for a mansion. They are lovely in the spring.

4 Casa del Guarda
The porter's lodge, one of two fairy-tale pavilions that guard the park entrance, is now an outpost of MUHBA, the Barcelona History Museum (p82). It contains an exhibition on the history of Park Güell.

UNFULFILLED IDEAS

Many of Gaudí's ideas for Park Güell were never realized owing to the economic failure of Eusebi Güell's garden city. Among the most daring of these ideas was his design for an enormous entrance gate.

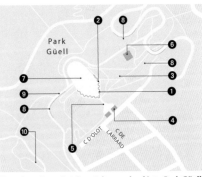

Two gingerbread-style gatehouses lead into Park Güell

across the city, and is fringed by the tiled bench. The square was originally called the Greek Theatre and was intended for open-air shows, with the audience watching from the surrounding terraces.

5 L'Escalinata del Drac

A fountain runs along the length of this tiled staircase, which is topped with whimsical creatures. The most famous of these is the multicoloured dragon, which has become a symbol of Barcelona.

6 Casa-Museu Gaudí

One of only two houses to be built in the park, this became Gaudí's home and contains original furnishings and memorabilia. It is located outside the Monumental Zone.

7 Plaça de la Natura

The park's main square offers panoramic views

8 Viaducts

Gaudí created three viaducts to serve as carriageways through Park Güell. Set into the steep slopes, and supported by archways and columns in the shape of waves or trees, they appear to emerge organically from the hill.

9 Pòrtic de la Bugadera

One of the park's many pathways, this is known as the Portico of the Laundress after the woman bearing a basket of washing on her head, carved into an arch.

10 Turó de les Tres Creus

Three crosses crown the very top of the hill, marking the spot where Gaudí and Güell, both intensely religious men, intended to build Park Güell's chapel. The climb to the top is well worth it in order to enjoy the spectacular city views.

Distinctive viaducts designed in the form of trees

LA PEDRERA

📍 E2 🏠 Pg de Gràcia 92 ⏰ Hours vary, chech website 🌐 lapedrera.com 🔗📍

Completed in 1912, this fantastic, undulating apartment block with its magical roof is one of the most emblematic of all Gaudí's works. Casa Milà, also known as La Pedrera ("the stone quarry"), was Gaudí's last great civic work before he dedicated himself to the Sagrada Família. Now restored to its former glory, La Pedrera contains the Espai Gaudí, an exhibition hall, courtyards, a terrace and the Pedrera Apartment.

1 Façade and Balconies

Defying the laws of gravity, La Pedrera's irreverent curved walls are held in place by rippling horizontal beams attached to invisible girders. Intricate wrought-iron balconies are an example of the artisan skill so integral to Modernisme.

2 Espai Gaudí

A series of drawings, photos, maquettes and multimedia displays help visitors grasp Gaudí's architectural wizardry. The museum is housed in the breathtaking vaulted attic, with its 270 gorgeous catenary brick arches forming atmospheric skeletal corridors.

3 Roof

The strikingly surreal rooftop sculpture park has chimneys resembling medieval warriors and huge ventilator ducts twisted into bizarre organic forms, not to mention wonderful views over the Eixample.

Huge, whimsical metal gates at the entrance

4 Gates

The mastery in imagining the wrought-iron gates reveals the influence of Gaudí's

The interior courtyard of El Patí de les Papallones

predecessors – four generations of artisan metal workers. The use of iron is integral to many of Gaudí's edifices.

5 El Patí de les Flors (The Flower Courtyard)

Like the first courtyard, this too has a grand, ornate staircase. This one is decorated with a stunning, floral ceiling painting.

6 El Patí de les Papallones (The Butterfly Courtyard)

A brigade of guides take visitors through this courtyard each day. A closer inspection

reveals its beautiful mosaics and multi-coloured wall paintings, which line a swirling, fairy-tale staircase.

7 Temporary Exhibition Hall

This interesting gallery space is run by the Catalunya-La Pedrera Foundation and hosts regular free art exhibitions. It has displayed works by Francis Bacon, Salvador Dalí and Marc Chagall among others. The ceiling here looks as if it has been coated with whisked egg whites.

8 La Pedrera Apartment

This Modernista flat with period furnishings is a reconstruction of a typical Barcelona bourgeois flat of the late 19th century. It provides an engaging contrast between the more sedate middle-class conservatism of the era and the undeniable wackiness of the outer building itself.

9 Auditorium

The auditorium, located in the former

GALLERY GUIDE

The Espai Gaudí, the Pedrera Apartment, the Pg de Gràcia and C/Provença Court-yards, the Exhibition Room and the roof are open to visitors. A lift goes up to the apartment, Espai Gaudí and the roof. The courtyards, staircases, café and shop are accessible from the entrance on the corner of Pg de Gràcia and C/Provença.

coach house, hosts regular events such as jazz and contemporary concerts. The adjacent garden offers visitors a glimpse of greenery.

10 La Pedrera Shop and Café

This has a wide range of Gaudí-related memorabilia, including replicas of the warrior chimneys in ceramic and bronze.

Enjoying the roof terrace at La Pedrera and (right) a reconstructed room

FUNDACIÓ JOAN MIRÓ

📍 B5 🏛 Av Miramar, Parc de Montjuïc ⏰ 10am–6pm Tue–Sun (Apr–Oct: to 8pm) 🌐 fmirobcn.org 🔗

Founded in 1975 by Joan Miró himself, who wanted it to be a centre of contemporary arts, this museum is now a superb tribute to a man whose legacy as an artist and a Catalan is visible across the city. It holds more than 14,000 of his artworks, tracing Miró's evolution from an innovative Surrealist in the 1920s to a modern artist in the 1960s.

Façade of the Fundació Joan Miró

1 Home i Dona Davant un Munt d'Excrements

Tortured and misshapen semi-abstract figures try to embrace against a black sky. Miró's pessimism at the time of *Man and Woman in Front of a Pile of Excrement* would soon be confirmed by the outbreak of the Civil War.

SHOP
The museum has a lovely gift shop, which offers an original and intriguing range of Miróesque curiosities, from tablecloths to champagne glasses.

2 Pagès Català al Clar de Lluna

The figurative painting *Catalan Peasant by Moonlight* dates from the late 1960s and highlights two of Miró's favourite themes: the earth and the night. The figure of the peasant, a simple collage of colour, is barely decipherable, as the crescent moon merges with his sickle and the night sky takes on the rich green tones of the earth.

3 L'Estel Matinal
This is one of 23 paintings known as the Constellation Series. The *Morning Star*'s introspective quality reflects Miró's state of mind at the outbreak of World War II, when he was hiding in Normandy. Spindly shapes of birds, women and heavenly bodies, as well as lines and planes of colour, are suspended in an undefined space.

4 Tapis de la Fundació
This immense, richly coloured tapestry represents the culmination of Miró's work with textiles, which began during the 1970s. The work framed the

Miró's huge *Tapis de la Fundació*

characteristic colour palette of Miró's output.

5 Sèrie Barcelona
The museum holds the only complete set of prints of this series of 50 black-and-white lithographs. This important collection is only occasionally on display.

6 Visiting Exhibitions
Over the years, a number of temporary exhibitions, which are usually held in the museum's west wing, have included retrospectives of high-profile artists such as Mark Rothko, Andy Warhol, René Magritte and Fernand Léger.

7 Font de Mercuri
Alexander Calder donated the *Mercury Fountain* to the Fundació as a mark of his friendship with Miró. The work was an anti-fascist tribute, conceived in memory of the attack on the town of Almadén.

8 Espai 13
This space showcases the experimental work of new artists from around the world. The exhibitions, based on a single theme each year, are usually radical and often use new technologies.

9 Terraces
More of Miró's sculptures are scattered on terraces, from which you can appreciate the Rationalist architecture of Josep Lluís Sert's geometric

EAT
The museum's elegant restaurant-café has a garden terrace with both indoor and outdoor seating. It's a great option for dining in the local area.

building. The 3-m-(10-ft-) tall *Caress of a Bird* (1967) dominates the terrace.

10 Sculpture Room
This room focuses on Miró's sculptures from the 1940s to the 1950s, when he experimented with ceramic, bronze and, later, painted media and found objects. Notable works include *Sun Bird* and *Moon Bird* (both 1946–9).

MUSEU PICASSO

P4 **C/Montcada 15–23** **10am–7pm Tue–Sun**
museu picasso.bcn.cat

Highlighting Pablo Picasso's (1881–1973) formative years, this museum houses the world's largest collection of his early works. At the age of 10, Picasso was already revealing remarkable artistic tendencies. In 1895, he moved to Barcelona and blossomed as an artist. The museum offers visitors the chance to discover the artist as he was discovering himself.

1 Home amb boina

This portrait reveals brush strokes – and a subject matter – that are far beyond a 13-year-old child. No puppies or cats for the young Picasso; instead, he painted the portraits of the oldest men in the village. He signed this work P Ruiz, because at this time he was still using his father's last name.

2 Autoretrat amb perruca

At 14, Picasso painted *Self-portrait with Wig*, a whimsical depiction of how he might have looked during the time of his artistic hero, Velázquez.

3 Ciència i Caritat

One of Picasso's first publicly exhibited paintings was *Science and Charity*. Picasso's father posed as the doctor.

4 L'Espera (Margot) and La Nana

Picasso's *Margot* is an evocative painting portraying a call girl as she waits for her next customer, while *La Nana* captures the defiant expression and stance of a heavily rouged dancer.

5 El Foll

The Madman is a fine example of Picasso's Blue period. This artistic phase, which lasted from 1901 to 1904, was characterized by melancholic themes and monochromatic, sombre colours.

6 Menu de Els Quatre Gats

Picasso's premier Barcelona exhibition was

Entrance to the Museu Picasso

 GALLERY GUIDE
The museum is housed in five medieval palaces that feature stone archways and pretty courtyards. The vast permanent collection is arranged chrono logically on the first and second floors of the first three palaces. The last two host temporary exhibitions on the first two floors.

EAT
The café in the museum offers a changing menu of tasty daily lunch specials. Grab a seat at one of the outdoor tables in summer.

held in 1900 at the Barri Gòtic café and centre of Modernisme, Els Quatre Gats. The artist's first commission was the pen-and-ink drawing of himself and a group of artist friends, which graced the menu cover of this bohemian hang-out.

7 Arlequí
A lifting of spirits led to Picasso's Neo-Classical period, typified by new paintings like *Arlequí* (*The Harlequin*). It depicted the dancer Léonide Massine and was a celebration of the light-hearted liberty of circus performers.

8 Home assegut
Works such as *Seated Man* confirmed Picasso's status as the greatest Analytic Cubist painter of the 20th century.

9 Las Meninas Series
Picasso's reverence for Velázquez culminated in this remarkable series of paintings, based on the Velázquez painting *Las Meninas*.

10 Cavall Banyegat
The anguished horse depicted in this graphite pencil drawing later appears in Picasso's large 1937 oil painting *Guernica*, which reveals the horrors of war. This work gives viewers the rare chance to observe the process that went into the creation of one of Picasso's most famous paintings.

Picasso's *Las Meninas, No.30,* painted in 1957

PALAU DE LA MÚSICA CATALANA

N2 **Sant Pere Més Alt** **palaumusica.cat**

Barcelona's Modernista movement reached its peak in Lluís Domènech i Montaner's magnificent 1908 concert hall. The lavish façade is ringed by mosaic pillars, and each part of the foyer in Domènech's "garden of music", from banisters to pillars, has a floral motif. The concert hall, whose height is the same as its breadth, is a celebration of natural forms, capped by a stained-glass dome that floods the space with sunlight.

1 Stained-Glass Ceiling

Topping the concert hall is a breathtaking, stained-glass inverted dome ceiling. By day, sunlight streams through the red and orange glass, illuminating the hall.

SHOP
The Palau shop sells items inspired by the building's architecture. It also has a section devoted to children.

2 Rehearsal Hall of the Orfeó Català

This semicircular, acoustically sound rehearsal room is a smaller version of the massive concert hall one floor above. At its centre is an inlaid foundation stone that commemorates the construction of the historic Palau.

3 Stained-Glass Windows

Blurring the boundaries between the outdoors and the interior, the architect encircled this concert hall with vast stained-glass windows decorated with floral designs that let in sunlight and reveal the changing time of day.

TOP TIP
Check out free live music performances on Café Palau's terrace.

4 Horse Sculptures

Charging from the ceiling are sculptor Eusebi Aranu's winged horses, infusing the concert hall with movement and verve. Also depicted is a representation of Wagner's chariot ride of the Valkyries, led by galloping horses that leap towards the stage.

5 Stage

The semicircular stage swarms with activity – even when

Ornate statues on the Palau's exterior

The concert hall at the Palau, a UNESCO World Heritage Site

no one's performing. Eighteen mosaic and terracotta muses spring from the backdrop, playing everything from the harp to the castanets.

6 Façade
The towering façade reveals Modernista delights on every level. An elaborate mosaic represents the Orfeó Català choral society, founded in 1891.

7 Foyer and Bar
Modernista architects worked with stone, wood, ceramic, marble and glass, all of which Domènech used liberally, most notably in the opulent foyer.

8 Lluís Millet Hall
Named after the iconic Catalan composer Lluís Millet,

this immaculately preserved lounge has gorgeous stained-glass windows. On the main balcony outside are rows of stunning mosaic pillars, each with a different design.

9 Busts
A bust of Catalan composer Josep Anselm Clavé (1824–74) marks the Palau's commitment to Catalan music. Facing him across the concert hall, a stern, unruly-haired Beethoven represents the hall's classical and international repertoire.

A stone bust of composer Beethoven

10 Concert and Dance Series
Over 500 concerts and dance shows are staged each year at the Palau de la Música Catalana, and seeing a show here is a thrilling experience. For symphonic concerts, keep an eye out for the Palau 100 series; for choral concerts, look out for the Orfeó Català series.

MUSEU D'ART CONTEMPORANI AND CENTRE DE CULTURA CONTEMPORÀNIA

MACBA: **K2** Pl dels Àngels Hours vary, chech website macba.cat; CCCB: **K1** C/Montalegre 5 11am–8pm Tue–Sun cccb.org

Barcelona's contemporary art museum stands in bold contrast to its surroundings. Established in 1995, the Museu d'Art Contemporani (MACBA), together with the Centre de Cultura Contemporània (CCCB) nearby, has played an integral part in the rejuvenation of El Raval.

1 Façade
The stark, geometrical façade of MACBA, designed by American Richard Meier, makes a startling impression against the dull and industrial-toned backdrop of this working-class neighbourhood. On the front side, hundreds of panes of glass reflect visitors and passersby.

2 Visiting Artist's Space
The *raison d'être* of MACBA is this flexible area showing the best in contemporary art. Past exhibitions have included Catalan artist Zush and Swiss painter Dieter Roth.

3 Revolving Permanent Collection
MACBA's permanent collection comprises more than 2,000 modern artworks, 10 per cent of which are on show at any one time. All major contemporary artistic trends are represented and the museum continues to expand its collection today, adding 150 new works in 2022.

4 Interior Corridors
Space and light are omnipresent in MACBA's bare white walkways, which hover between floors. Look through the glass panels onto the Plaça dels Àngels for myriad images before you even enter the gallery spaces.

TOP TIP

MACBA has tours in sign language and adapted tours for the visually impaired.

MACBA aglow with colourful lights at night

5 Capella MACBA
One of the few surviving Renaissance chapels in Barcelona has been converted for use as MACBA's temporary exhibition space. It is located in a former convent across the Plaça dels Àngels.

6 A Sudden Awakening
One of the only artworks on permanent display in MACBA is Antoni Tàpies' deconstructed bed (1992–3), with its bedding flung across the wall in disarray. Its prominence underlines Tàpies' importance to Catalan modern art.

7 Thinking and Reading Spaces
Pleasant and unusual features of MACBA are

EAT
Pause at the nearby Doña Rosa café (C/Ferlandina), which offers modern Mediterranean food, or at the delightful terrace cafés in MACBA and CCCB.

the white leather sofas between the galleries. Usually next to a shelf of relevant books and a set of headphones, these quiet spaces provide the perfect resting spot to contemplate – and learn more about – the art.

8 El Pati de les Dones/CCCB
This courtyard off Carrer Montalegre forms part of the neighbouring CCCB. A prismatic screen acts as a mirror reflecting the medieval courtyard, giving visitors a magical juxtaposition of different architectural styles.

9 Plaça Joan Coromines
The contrast between the modern MACBA, the university building, the Tuscan-style CCCB and the 19th-century mock-Romanesque church make this one of the city's most interesting squares.

10 Temporary Exhibitions/CCCB
Exhibitions at the CCCB tend to be more theme-based than artist-specific. It hosts the World Press Photo exhibition in spring and numerous literary festivals throughout the year. Home to several fascinating avant-garde art exhibits, the CCCB is always at the forefront of the latest cultural trends.

Clockwise from right **Antoni Tàpies'** *A Sudden Awakening;* **spartan white corridors connecting the MACBA's floors; walking past the CCCB's glass façade**

TOP 10 OF EVERYTHING

Sagrada Família

CHURCHES AND CHAPELS

Rose window at the Basílica de Santa Maria del Mar

1 Basílica de Santa Maria del Mar

The elegant church *(p82)* of Santa Maria del Mar (1329–83) is one of the finest examples of Catalan Gothic, a style characterized by simplicity. A spectacular stained-glass rose window illuminates the lofty interior.

2 Barcelona Cathedral

Barcelona's magnificent Gothic cathedral *(p28)* has an eye-catching façade and a peaceful cloister.

3 Temple Expiatori del Sagrat Cor

📍 B1 📌 Pl del Tibidabo 📞 93 417 56 86 ⏰ Crypt (lower church): 9am–8pm daily (Apr, May & Sep: to 9pm; Jun–Aug: to 9:30pm); upper church and terrace: hours vary, call ahead ♿

Mount Tibidabo is an appropriate perch for this over-the-top Neo-Gothic church *(p121)*, topped with a large golden statue of Christ with arms outstretched. The name of the mountain comes from the words *tibidabo*, meaning "I shall give you", said to have been uttered by the Devil in his temptation of Christ. The priest here celebrates the Eucharist throughout the day.

4 Església de Sant Pau del Camp

Founded as a Benedictine monastery in the 9th century by Guifre II, a count of Barcelona, this elegant church *(p93)* was rebuilt the following century. Its sculpted façade and intimate cloister with rounded arches exemplify the Romanesque style.

5 Església de Sant Pere de les Puelles

📍 P2 📌 Pl de Sant Pere ⏰ 10am–8pm daily (to 6pm Sun)

Built in 801 as a chapel for troops stationed in Barcelona, this *església* later became a spiritual retreat for young noblewomen. The church was rebuilt in the 1100s and is notable for its Romanesque central cupola and a series of capitals with carved leaves. Look out for two stone tablets depicting a Greek cross, which are from the original chapel.

6 Basílica de Santa Maria del Pi

📍 L3 📌 Pl del Pi ⏰ 10am–6pm Mon–Sat ♿

This lovely Gothic church with its ornate stained-glass windows

races the Plaça del Pi *(p53)*. The rose window is one of the largest in Catalonia.

7 Capella de Sant Miquel and Església al Monestir de Pedralbes

Accessed through an arch set in ancient walls, the gorgeous Monestir de Pedralbes *(p119)*, founded in 1327, still has the air of a closed community. Inside is a Gothic cloister and the Capella de Sant Miquel, decorated with murals by Catalan artist Ferrer Bassa in 1346. The adjoining Gothic church contains the alabaster tomb of Queen Elisenda, the monastery's founder. On the church side, her effigy wears royal robes and on the other, a nun's habit.

8 Capella de Santa Àgata
N3 Pl del Rei 10am–2pm & 5–8pm Tue–Sun

Within the beautiful Palau Reial is the medieval Capella de Santa Àgata, which can only be entered as part of a visit to the Museu d'Història de Barcelona *(p82)*. The 15th-century altarpiece is by Jaume Huguet. Entry is free from 3 to 5pm on Sundays.

9 Capella de Sant Jordi
M4 Pl Sant Jaume 2nd and 4th weekend of the month

In the Palau de la Generalitat *(p81)* is this fine 15th-century chapel, dedicated to the patron saint of Catalonia.

10 Església de Betlem
La Rambla *(p26)* was once dotted with religious buildings, most dating to the 17th and 18th centuries. This Baroque *església* is one of the major functioning churches from this period. Immensely popular around Christmas, it hosts one of the largest displays of *pessebres* (manger scenes) in the world.

Stunning façade of the Basilica de Santa Maria del Pi

MUSEUMS AND GALLERIES

1 Fundació Joan Miró
The airy, high-ceilinged galleries of this splendid museum (p36) are a fitting home for the bold, abstract works of Joan Miró, one of Catalonia's most acclaimed 20th-century artists. The works on display include sketches, paintings, ceramics and textiles.

2 Museu Nacional d'Art de Catalunya
Discover Catalonia's Romanesque and Gothic heritage at this impressive museum (p30), housed in the 1929 Palau Nacional. Highlights include striking medieval frescoes and a collection of Modernista furnishings and artworks.

3 Museu Picasso
Witness the budding – and meteoric rise – of Picasso's artistic genius at this unique museum (p38). With over 5,000 artworks, the Museu Picasso has one of the world's largest collections of the painter's early works.

4 Museu d'Art Contemporani and Centre de Cultura Contemporània
Inaugurated in 1995, MACBA (p42) is Barcelona's centre for modern art. Together with the neighbouring CCCB, these sites form an artistic and cultural hub in the heart of El Raval. Both regularly host temporary exhibitions: the MACBA showcases contemporary artists; the CCCB is more theme-based.

5 Fundació Tàpies
Works by Catalan artist Antoni Tàpies are showcased in this graceful Modernista building (p112). Venture inside to discover Tàpies' rich repertoire, from early collage works to large abstract paintings, many alluding to political and social themes.

6 Museu d'Història de Barcelona (MUHBA)
Explore the medieval Palau Reial and wander among the splendid remains of Barcelona's Roman walls and waterways at the city's history museum (p82). The museum is partly housed in the 15th-century Casa Padellàs on the impressive medieval Plaça del Rei.

7 Museu Frederic Marès
Catalan sculptor Frederic Marès (1893–1991) was a passionate and eclectic collector. Housed here (p83), under one roof, are many remarkable finds amassed during his travels. Among the vast array of historical objects on display are Romanesque and Gothic religious art and sculptures, plus everything from dolls and fans to pipes and walking sticks.

8 Museu del FC Barcelona
This shrine to the city's famous football club houses trophies, posters and memorabilia that celebrate the club's long history. It can only be visited in combination with a tour of the adjacent Camp Nou Stadium (p120). There are also immersive tours of the museum, with interactive experiences.

The FC Barcelona crest, first designed in 1949

A replica of Don Juan of Austria's galley the *Real* at Museu Marítim

9 Museu Marítim

The formidable seafaring history of Barcelona is showcased in the cavernous, 13th-century Drassanes Reials (Royal Shipyards). The extensive collection *(p91)*, which ranges from the Middle Ages to the 19th century, includes a full-scale replica of the *Real*, the flagship galley of Don Juan of Austria, who led the Christians to victory against the Turks at the Battle of Lepanto in 1571. Also on display are model ships, maps and navigational instruments. Several guided tours take visitors around the museum.

10 CosmoCaixa Museu de la Ciència

Exhibits covering the whole history of science, from the Big Bang to the computer age, are housed in this modern museum *(p120)*. Highlights include an interactive tour of the geological history of our planet, an area of real Amazonian rainforest along with a planetarium. The geological section showcases a wide range of plant and animal fossils. Don't miss the temporary displays on environmental issues as well as the family activities.

TOP 10
QUIRKY MUSEUMS AND MONUMENTS

1. Museu de Cera
🔲 L5 🔲 Ptge de la Banca 7
Home to over 350 wax figures including Marilyn Monroe, General Franco and Antoni Gaudí.

2. Hash, Marihuana and Hemp Museum
🔲 E5 🔲 C/Ample 35
This cannabis museum is set in a magnificent Modernista building.

3. Casa dels Entremeses
🔲 N3 🔲 Pl Beates 2
Traditional Catalan puppets such as gegants (giants) and capgrossos (fatheads) are found here.

4. Moco Museum
🔲 P4 🔲 C/Montcada 25
This modern art museum *(p84)* features works by artists such as Andy Warhol and Banksy. The digital installations on display are excellent.

5. Museu dels Autòmates
🔲 B1 🔲 Parc d'Atraccions del Tibidabo
A colourful museum of human and animal automatons.

6. Museu de la Xocolata
🔲 P4 🔲 C/Comerç 36
A celebration of chocolate; enjoy interactive exhibits, edible city models and tastings.

7. Museu del Disseny
🔲 H3 🔲 Pl de les Glòries Catalanes
A design museum *(p113)* focusing on the themes of clothes, architecture, objects and graphic design.

8. Museu del Perfum
🔲 E2 🔲 Pg de Gràcia 39
This intriguing museum displays perfume bottles from Roman times to the present.

9. Cap de Barcelona
🔲 N5 🔲 Pg de Colom
Pop artist Roy Lichtenstein's *Barcelona Head*, created for the 1992 Olympics.

10. Peix
🔲 G5 🔲 Port Olímpic
Frank Gehry's huge shimmering goldfish sculpture (1992).

MODERNISTA BUILDINGS

1 Sagrada Família
Dizzying spires and intricate sculptures adorn Gaudí's masterpiece *(p22)*. Construction began at the height of Modernisme, but is still in progress more than a century later.

2 La Pedrera
This apartment block *(p34)*, with its curving façade and bizarre rooftop, has all of Gaudí's architectural trademarks. Especially characteristic are the building's wrought-iron balconies and the ceramic mosaics decorating the entrance halls.

3 Fundació Tàpies
With a Rationalist, plain façade alleviated only by its Mudéjar-style brickwork, this building *(p112)*, dating from 1886, was home to the publishing house Montaner i Simón. It was the first Modernista work to be designed by Domènech i Montaner, which explains why it has so few of the ornate decorative touches that distinguish his later works. Today it is home to the Fundació Tàpies, and is dominated by an enormous sculpture by the Catalan artist.

4 Sant Pau Recinte Modernista
In defiant contrast to the Eixample's symmetrical grid-like pattern, this ambitious project *(p111)* was planned around two avenues running at 45-degree angles to the Eixample streets. Started by Domènech i Montaner in 1905 and completed by his son in 1930, the Hospital de la Santa Creu i de Sant Pau's pavilions are lavishly embellished with mosaics, stained glass and sculptures by Eusebi Arnau. The octagonal columns with floral capitals are inspired by those in the Monestir de Santes Creus *(p130)*, to the south of Barcelona.

5 Casa Batlló
⬛ E2 🏠 Pg de Gràcia 43 🕐 9am–8pm daily 🌐 casabatllo.es ♿
Illustrating Gaudí's nationalist sentiments, Casa Batlló, on La Mansana de la Discòrdia *(p111)*, is a striking representation of the Sant Jordi story *(p47)*. The roof is the dragon's back; the balconies, in the form of carnival masks, are the skulls of the dragon's victims. The façade exemplifies Gaudí's remarkable use of colour and texture.

6 Casa Amatller
⬛ E2 🏠 Pg de Gràcia 41 🕐 10am–6pm daily for guided and audio tours only 🌐 amatller.org ♿ 🔲
The top of Casa Amatller's façade bursts into a brilliant display of blue, cream and pink tiles with burgundy florets. Architect Puig i Cadafalch's

lendid entrance of the
nt Pau Recinte Modernista

aggerated decorative use of ceramics
typical of Modernisme. Tours include
e Modernista apartment and a slide
ow in Amatller's former photography
idio, along with showcasing the
o-Medieval vestibule.

Casa de les Punxes
(Casa Terradas)
Av Diagonal 420 W casales
nxes.com

king Modernisme's Gothic and
edieval obsessions to extremes that
hers seldom dared, Puig i Cadafalch
eated this imposing, castle-like
ucture between 1903 and 1905
12). While the building is named after
original owners, the Terradas family,
has acquired the nickname Casa de
Punxes or "House of Spines" because
the sharp, needle-like spires that rise
from its conical turrets. The flamboy-
t spires contrast with a façade that is
arsely decorated. The building is now
ed as a co-working space.

Palau Güell
The use of parabolic arches
re *(p91)* to orchestrate space is

an example of Gaudí's experiments with
structure. He also used unusual building
materials, such as ebony and rare South
American woods. The palace has a permanent exhibition of the furniture that
was once used by its original residents,
the Güell family.

9 Casa Vicens
A UNESCO World Heritage Site,
Casa Vicens *(p121)* was the first home
designed by Antoni Gaudí. The
façade is an explosion of colour, at
once austere and flamboyant, with
Neo-Mudéjar elements and sgraffito
floral motifs. The building now functions as a cultural centre. Inside,
you will find perfectly preserved
residential rooms with original furniture and paintings. Down in the
coal cellar is a fascinating underground bookshop.

10 Palau de la Música
Catalana
Domènech i Montaner's magnificent
concert hall is a joyous celebration
of Catalan music *(p40)*. Ablaze with
mosaic friezes, stained glass, ceramics
and sculptures, it displays Modernista
style in its full glory. The work of Miquel
Blay on the façade is rated as one of
the best examples of Modernista
sculpture in Barcelona.

ulted ceilings of the former stables
Palau Güell's basement

PUBLIC SQUARES

1 Plaça de Catalunya
⬙ M1

Barcelona's nerve centre is the huge Plaça de Catalunya, a lively hub from which the city's activity seems to radiate. This square is most visitors' first real glimpse of Barcelona. The airport bus stops here, as do RENFE trains and countless metro and bus lines, including most night buses, and the tourist information office is located here. The square's commercial swagger is evident all around, headed by Spain's omnipresent department store, El Corte Inglés. Pigeons flutter haphazardly at the square's centre and travellers wander about. Crowds flock to see the concerts that are held in the square during festivals.

2 Plaça Reial
The arcaded Plaça Reial (p82), in the heart of the Barri Gòtic, is unique among Barcelona's public squares due to its old-world charm, gritty urbanization and Neo-Classical flair. It is home not only to fascinating Gaudí lampposts and majestic mid-19th-century buildings, but also to a slew of buzzing bars and cafés, and an entertaining and colourful crowd of inner-city Barcelona denizens.

3 Plaça del Rei
⬙ N4

One of the city's best-preserved medieval squares, the Barri Gòtic's Plaça del Rei is ringed by grand historic buildings. Among them is the 14th-century Palau Reial (p82), which houses the Saló del Tinell, a spacious Catalan Gothic throne room and banqueting hall.

4 Plaça de Sant Jaume
Laden with power and history, this is the administrative heart (p81) of modern-day Barcelona. The plaça is flanked by the city's two key government buildings, the stately Palau de la Generalitat and the 15th-century Ajuntament.

5 Plaça de la Vila de Gràcia
⬙ E1

The progressive, vibrant area of Gràcia, a former village annexed by Barcelona in 1897, still exudes a small-town ambience where socializing with the neighbours means heading for the nearest plaça. Topping the list is this atmospheric square, with an impressive clock tower rising at its centre. Bustling outdoor cafés draw buskers and a sociable crowd.

ns of the Roman necropolis
laça de la Vila de Madrid

Plaça de la Vila de Madrid
12

ew steps from the busy
Rambla *(p26)* is this spacious
ça, graced with the remains of
oman necropolis. A remnant
Roman Barcino, the square sat
t beyond the boundaries of
walled Roman city. A row of
adorned 2nd- to 4th-century
nbs was discovered here in
57. The complete remains can
viewed from street level.

Plaça Comercial
P4

e buzzing Passeig del Born
minates in Plaça Comercial, an
iting square dotted with cafés
d bars. It faces the 19th-century
rn Market *(p82)*, which has
en transformed into a cultural
ntre and exhibition space.

Plaça de Santa Maria
N5

is beautiful square in the El Born
trict gets its name from the
gnificent 15th-century Basílica
Santa Maria del Mar *(p82)*, which
minates it. Bask in its Gothic
bience, people-watch and soak
the sun at one of the outdoor
rrace cafés.

o-Classical Plaça Reial, one of
rcelona's most popular squares

9 Plaça del Sol
F1

Tucked within the cosy grid of Gràcia, this square, popularly called Plaça del Encants, is surrounded by handsome 19th-century buildings. As evening descends, it transforms into one of the most lively spots for after-dark festivities, and you can join all the *Barcelonins* who come here to mingle on the outdoor terraces.

10 Plaça de Sant Josep Oriol and Plaça del Pi
M3 & L3

Old-world charm meets modern café culture in the Barri Gòtic's leafy Plaça de Sant Josep Oriol and Plaça del Pi, named after the pine trees (*pi* in Catalan) that shade its nooks and crannies. Plaça de Sant Josep Oriol is a common haunt for Barcelona's street artists and its medieval neighbour, Plaça del Pi, is lined with stunning Baroque structures. The lovely Gothic church of Santa Maria del Pi *(p46)* is set between the two squares.

PARKS AND BEACHES

1 Parc de Cervantes

🏠 Av Diagonal 708 🕐 10am– dush daily

Built in 1964 to celebrate 25 years of Franco's rule, this beautiful park on the outskirts of Barcelona would have been more appropriately named Park of the Roses. There are over 11,000 rose bushes of 245 varieties; when in bloom, their scent pervades the entire park. Visitors pour in at weekends, but the park is blissfully deserted during the week.

2 Park Güell

The twisting pathways and avenues of columned arches of Park Güell *(p32)* blend in with the lush hillside, playfully fusing nature and fantasy to create an urban paradise. From the esplanade, with its stunning mosaic bench, visitors have spectacular views of the city and of the fairy-tale gatehouses below.

3 Parc del Laberint d'Horta

Dating back to 1791, the enchanting Parc del Laberint d'Horta *(p120)* is among the city's oldest gardens. Situated above the city, where the air is cooler and cleaner, the park includes themed gardens, waterfalls and a small canal. The highlight is the vast maze with a statue of Eros at its centre. There's a picnic area and a children's playground at the entrance to the gardens.

4 Jardins de Joan Brossa

🏠 Plaça de Dante 🕐 10am– dush daily

Set on the flanks of the Montjuïc hill, the Jardins de Joan Brossa *(p102)* is named after the renowned Catalan poet and offers a serene escape with spectacular glimpses of the city below. Paths wind through leafy groves, dotted with whimsical musical instruments and playgrounds (including a little zip line) that will delight children.

5 Parc de la Ciutadella

The largest landscaped park in Barcelona *(p106)* offers a refreshingly green, tranquil antidote to city life. Once the location of the 18th-century military citadel, this lovely, serene 19th-century park is now home to the Catalan parliament, a placid boating lake and a variety of works by Catalan sculptors as well as modern artists. It also has the extravagant Cascada Monumental, a two-tiered fountain, which Gaudí helped design.

the well-maintained garden of the 18th-century Parc del Laberint d'Horta

6 Parc de l'Espanya Industrial

C/Muntadas 37 ⏰ 10am– midnight daily

Located on the site of a former textile factory, this park was built in 1986 by Basque architect Luis Peña Ganchegui. It is an appealing recreational space, with 10 lighthouse-style viewing towers lined along one side of the lake and an enormous cast-iron dragon that doubles as a slide. There is a good terrace bar with a playground for kids.

7 City Beaches

The beaches (p105) of Barcelona underwent a radical face-lift during the 1992 Olympics. Today, the stretches of the Port Olímpic and Barceloneta, a short hop on the metro from the city centre, are a people magnet. The beaches are regularly cleaned and the facilities include showers, toilets, play areas for kids, volleyball nets and an open-air gym. Boats and surfboards can be hired. Be aware, though, that incidents of bag snatching are common.

8 Castelldefels

Just 20 km (12 miles) south of the city are 5 km (3 miles) of wide sandy

beaches with shallow waters, ideal for watersports (windsurfing boards are available for hire). Beach bars entice weekend sun worshippers out of the afternoon sun for long, lazy seafood lunches and jugs of sangria. Take a train to Platja de Castelldefels from Estació de Sants or Passeig de Gràcia to reach these beaches.

9 Parc de Joan Miró

B2 C/Tarragona 74 ⏰ 10am–dusk daily

Also known as Parc de l'Escorxador, this park in Eixample was built on the site of a 19th-century slaughterhouse (escorxador). Dominating the paved upper level of the park is Miró's striking 22-m (72-ft) sculpture *Dona i Ocell* (*Woman and Bird*), created in 1983. There are several play areas for kids and a couple of kiosk cafés.

10 Premià de Mar and El Masnou

Arguably the best set of beaches within easy reach of Barcelona, lie just 20 km (12 miles) to the north of the city. Hop on a train to Premià or El Masnou from Plaça de Catalunya or Estació de Sants to get there. These two adjoining beaches attract locals and visitors alike with stunning golden sand and clear, blue waters.

Windsurfing along the sandy beaches of Castelldefels

OFF THE BEATEN TRACK

2 Jardins de la Rambla de Sants

⊞ A2 ⊞ C/d'Antoni de Capmany s/n
This elevated park, which stretches for almost a kilometre from the Plaça de Sants to the La Bordeta district, is built above a disused railway track. It provides a peaceful stroll, with some refreshing bursts of greenery in among the high-rise apartment blocks and old factory buildings.

3 El Refugi 307

⊞ C5 ⊞ C/Nou de la Rambla 175
ⓦ barcelona.cat/museuhistoria/en/heritages ⊞ ⊞
More than a thousand underground shelters were built beneath the city during the Spanish Civil War, when Barcelona was being bombed by the nationalist forces. Shelter 307, with 400 m (1,300 ft) of tunnels, contained an infirmary, a toilet, a water fountain, a fireplace and a children's room. It is now part of the Museu d'Història de Barcelona (p82) and provides a glimpse into the torment endured by city residents during the war. Book ahead for tours in English, which take place on Sundays.

1 Bunkers del Carmel

⊞ C1 ⊞ C/del Turó de la Rovira s/n
Barcelona has a handful of disused bunkers – a reminder of the aerial attacks that took place during the long Spanish Civil War. Chiselled into the side of a hill in the El Carmel district is Bunkers del Carmel. The roof at this site acts as a viewing platform, with a perfect vista of the city at the golden hour. The bunker closes at sunset, but the park around it also offers stunning views.

Enjoying impressive city views from Bunkers del Carmel

Mercat de la Llibertat

📍 Pl Llibertat 27 📞 93 413 23 23
8:30am–8:30pm Mon–Fri, 8:30am–3pm Sat; stalls hours may vary

The Mercat de la Llibertat in Gràcia was built in 1888 and is notable for its beautiful wrought-iron and ceramic decoration. The square where it stands was once known as the Plaça de la Constitució and was used as a farmer's market. As well as a fabulous range of fresh produce, today it also has excellent stalls selling such items as original photographs, kitchenware and various styles of clothes.

5 Parc del Laberint d'Horta

These lovely 18th-century gardens (p120) are filled with classical statuary, small pavilions and ornamental ponds, but it is the fabulous and surprisingly tricky maze at their heart that is the big draw.

6 Convent de Sant Agustí

📍 P3 📍 Pl l'Academia s/n, C/Comerç 36 🕙 9am–10pm Mon–Fri, 10am–2pm & 4–9pm Sat

The 15th-century Convent de Sant Agustí is now a cultural centre, with a pretty little café underneath the arches of what remains of the cloister. Relaxed and family-friendly, it is a great place to spend an afternoon.

7 Basílica de la Puríssima Concepció

📍 F2 📍 C/d'Aragó 299 🕙 7:30am–1pm & 5–9pm Mon–Fri (Aug: to 8pm); 7:30am–2pm & 5–9pm Sun
🌐 parroquiaconcepciobcn.org

Dating back to the 13th century, this basilica was originally part of the Santa Maria de Jonqueres monastery. It was moved stone by stone to its current site in the 19th century. Head for the charming Gothic cloister, which is filled with greenery and birdsong, and bordered by slender 15th-century columns. The basilica regularly hosts concerts.

The wrought-iron gates of the Güell Pavilions, featuring the iconic dragon

8 Güell Pavilions

📍 B2 📍 Av Pedralbes 7 📞 93 317 76 52 🕙 10am–4pm daily

Gaudí designed the gatehouses and stable, known collectively as the Güell Pavilions (p32), for his patron Eusebi Güell in the 1880s. You can admire the enormous dragon, inspired by the myth of the Garden of the Hesperides, which lunges out of the wrought-iron gate, and visit the complex as part of a guided tour; English tours take place at 10am, 11am and 3pm.

9 Plaça Osca

📍 B2

This leafy old square in the Sants neighbourhood is flanked by cafés and bars, with tables spilling out onto the pavements. Rarely frequented by tourists but increasingly popular with trendy locals, the square has a clutch of great spots to enjoy artisan beer and some organic tapas.

10 Parc de Cervantes

Every spring, hundreds of people converge on the gardens in the Parc de Cervantes (p54) to admire the blooms of 11,000 rose bushes of 245 varieties. Grassy lawns extend around the rose gardens, dotted with picnic areas and children's playgrounds.

FAMILY ATTRACTIONS

Enjoying a thrilling ride at the Parc d'Atraccions del Tibidabo

1 Parc d'Atraccions del Tibidabo

With its old-fashioned rides, the only surviving funfair *(p119)* in the city is a delight. The attractions include a roller coaster, a House of Horrors, bumper cars, a Ferris wheel and the Museu dels Autòmates *(p49)*, with animatronics of all shapes and sizes. There's also a puppet show, picnic areas, playgrounds, and plenty of cafés and restaurants.

2 La Rambla

Your shoulders will be aching from carrying the kids high above the crowds by the time you reach the end of Barcelona's main boulevard *(p26)*. Fire eaters, buskers, human statues dressed up as Greek goddesses – you name it and it's likely to be keeping the hordes entertained on La Rambla.

3 Museu Marítim

Ancient maps showing monster-filled seas, restored fishing boats and a collection of ships' figureheads give a taste of the city's maritime history. Well worth a look is the full-size Spanish galleon complete with sound and light effect Set in the vast former medieval ship-yards, the Drassanes, this museum *(p91)* is an absolute must for any budding sea captain.

4 Parc de l'Oreneta
🅿 A1 🚂 Tren de l'Oreneta

This delightful, shaded park has a variety of paths winding up the hillsid lots of play parks and picnic areas, an a paddock where kids can take pony rides. Perhaps the best of all is the miniature train Tren de l'Oreneta *(trenoreneta.com)*, which makes a 650-m (2,130-ft) lap around the park from a tiny train station.

5 Parc del Laberint d'Horta

The highlight of this exceptionally beautiful park *(p120)* is the huge hedg maze where children can live out all of their *Alice in Wonderland* fantasies. There's a play area on the grounds, which is great fun for the kids, and a bar for grown-ups. The park is usually busy on Sundays.

6 Telefèric de Montjuïc

◻ C5 ◻ Parc de Montjuïc
◷ 10am–6pm daily (Mar–May &
Oct: to 7pm; Jun–Sep: to 9pm)
◻ telefericdemontjuic.cat ◻

Instead of taking the nerve-jangling cable-car ride across the port, try these smaller, lower-altitude cable-car trips if you have children with you. The ride to the Montjuïc summit also has the added appeal of the castle (p99) at the top, which history lovers will find fascinating, with cannons for the kids to clamber on.

7 City Beaches

For kids, there's more to going to the beach in Barcelona than just splashing in warm waters and frolicking in the sand. The Port Vell and Port Olímpic platges (beaches) offer a good choice of well-equipped play areas to keep the little ones entertained (p105). Numerous bars and restaurants make finding refreshment easy, too.

8 FC Barcelona Museum and Stadium Tour

Football fans can follow in the footsteps of their favourite players at the FC Barcelona Museum and

Stadium Tour (p120). See the changing rooms where the player prepare, explore the legendary stadium and get hands-on with interactive displays. Barça's impressive array of trophies are another big draw.

9 Museu d'Història de Catalunya

This wonderful museum (p105) traces Catalonia's history through a range of interactive exhibits that make it a very popular hit with Catalan school groups and visitors of all ages. Visitors can dress up as medieval knights and gallop around on wooden horses. In addition to its stock of children's activities, the museum hosts an exciting story hour every Saturday wherein Catalan legends are re-enacted.

10 Boat Trips

The city's charming "swallow boats", Las Golondrinas (p106) make regular sightseeing trips out of the port, providing a fun excursion for older children. Younger kids will probably prefer messing about in a rowing boat on the lake at the Parc de la Ciutadella (p106).

Rowing across calm waters in Parc De La Ciutadella

NIGHTS OUT

1 Jazz Clubs
Barcelona's jazz scene is globally-famous. But don't take our word for it, take it from the thousands who attend the annual Barcelona International Jazz Festival (p75), where the greatest acts in the world perform. Year round, there are also nightly performances at legendary jazz bars like Jamboree (jamboree-jazz.com) and Harlem (harlemjazzclub.es).

2 Cinemas
A city fit for the silver screen, Barcelona has plenty of places to entice cinephiles. Check out the art films, retrospectives and events at Filmoteca (filmoteca.cat), the Catalan film institute, while for independent fare visit the Verdi cinema (barcelona.cines-verdi.com) in Gràcia. For films in their original language, look for "VO" in the listings.

3 Night clubs
Barcelona is a city full of rhythm and when the sun goes down, its denizens start to dance. Listen to everything from electronica to indie pop across the five areas of the legendary Razzmatazz (sala razzmatazz.com) or enjoy remixes and celeb spotting at the Sutton Club (sutton barcelona.com), the most exclusive club in the city. Just be sure to pace yourself – many clubs don't open before midnight.

4 LGBTQ+ Nights Out
Barcelona is one of the most LGBTQ+-friendly cities in Europe, and the community's fun-loving centre can be found in the part of Eixample around Carrer Balmes, the Gran Via, Carrer Urgell and Carrer Aragó. Enter the warm embrace of this wonderfully welcoming area and lose yourself in the many bars, clubs and restaurants found here, from established venues like PuntoBCN (C/ de Muntaner, 65) to miniature discobars like La Carra (lacarrabcn.com).

5 Comedy shows
Looking for a laugh? Whether it's stand-up, improv or open-mic nights, Barcelona's burgeoning comedy scene is a great way to spend an evening. Teatreneu (teatreneu.com) is where you can get to know the city's funny bone, with great comedians performing in mainly Spanish or Catalan. For English fare, try The Comedy Clubhouse (thecomedyclubhouse.es), which pairs traditional stand-up with more unique shows, such as drunk comedy debates.

6 Cocktail Bars
If you think Barcelona is all about sangria, you'd be very much mistaken. Cocktails are a huge part of the city's nightlife, where you'll find some of the world's best bars and finest mixologists. Sip the James Bond-themed cocktails at Solange (p115) or try the regularly changing menu at Two Shmucks (p96).

7 Theatre
Barcelona is a city with a flourishing theatre scene, which ranges from classic productions to avant-garde performances, with many of the best shows found at the elegant Teatre Nacional de Catalunya (tnc.cat) and the Teatre

A live performance at Tablao Flamenco Cordobes

Trentemøller performing live at Razzmatazz nightclub

liure (teatrelliure.com). Here in summer? Head to the Festival Grec de Barcelona for open-air shows at the beautiful Teatre Grec (p100).

8 Sunset cruises
As dusk settles over the sea, the waters off Barcelona are the perfect place to see the sun set behind the city. Those looking to unwind after a long day should jump aboard the catamaran Orsom (barcelona-orsom.com). Here, you can kick back on deck and soak up those last rays of sun as you cruise along the coast, to a soundtrack of smooth jazz.

9 Opera and Zarzuela
You'll find no shortage of opera among the spectacular concert venues in Barcelona. The best are found at the Gran Teatre del Liceu (p26), the oldest theatre in Barcelona, while the Auditori (auditori.cat) also features opera among its varied programme. For something different, look out for the occasional zarzuela (Spanish light opera) shows at these venues, which combine operatic music with dance and spoken dialogue.

10 Flamenco
Flamenco may have originated in Andalucía in the south of Spain, but there is a passionate following in Catalonia, with local flamenco lovers flocking to see the flamenco tablaos shows ("flamenco floorboards"). Visit Tablao Cordobes (tablaocordobes.es) to see emerging talents alongside the best contemporary artists, including Miguel Poveda and the legendary Mayte Martín.

TOP 10 CATALAN ENTERTAINMENT STARS

1. Rosalia
Rosalia is a world-famous musician and singer who combines flamenco with other musical genres to create a wholly unique genre of her own.

2. Montserrat Caballé
One of the greatest opera singers ever, Caballé won scores of awards and famously sang Barcelona with Freddie Mercury for the 1992 Olympic Games.

3. Daniel Brühl
Barcelona-born Brühl is has given spectacular performances in films such as Good Bye, Lenin!, Inglourious Basterds and Rush.

4. Laia Costa
Costa is one of the most famous actors in Spain who has starred in Victoria, Lullaby, Newness and Un Amor, among others.

5. Maite Martin
Maite Martin is a pioneering Catalan flamenco singer, renowned for her powerful voice.

6. Clara Segura
An accomplished actress, Clara Segura is known to international audiences for her role in the Oscar-winning film The Sea Inside.

7. Àlex Brendemühl
Brendemühl played Josef Mengele in The German Doctor, among over 60 other films and TV roles.

8. David Verdaguer
An award-winning Catalan actor, David Verdaguer is most famous for 10,000 km, which earned him a Gaudí Award.

9. Morad
Morad is a Catalan rapper and singer known for his energetic and raw style; his music features a blend of catchy beats and bold lyrics.

10. Joan Manuel Serrat
The most celebrated Catalan singer, Serrat combines lyricism and poetry with an eclectic style. He was a famous critic of the Francoist dictatorship.

PHOTO SPOTS

1 Font Màgica
You can take some truly extraordinary photos of Barcelona's enchanting and exuberant "Magic Fountain" *(p99)*, which is linked by a long, choreographed line of smaller fountains all the way up to the Palau Nacional *(p99)*. Due to the ongoing drought in Catalonia, the brilliantly colourful night show has been suspended but it is hoped that it will be reinstated in the near future.

2 Rooftop of the Barcelona Cathedral
For a bird's-eye view of the narrow, winding lanes and alleys of Barri Gòtic *(p80)*, climb up to the roof terrace of the Barcelona Cathedral *(p28)*, where gargoyles and the carved stone of the central spire vie for attention.

3 Museu d'Història de Catalunya
The café on the top floor of the Museu d'Història de Catalunya *(p105)* offers dazzling views over the yacht-filled Port Vell and up to the slopes of Montjuïc *(p98)*. It is a good idea to come at dusk to capture some of the best photos of Barcelona.

The 18th-century Plaça de Sant Felip Neri at dusk

4 Plaça de Sant Felip Neri
The labyrinthine alleys and squares that make up Barri Gòtic *(p80)*, plus the numerous historical notes found in among them, are a photographer's dream. The little Plaça de Sant Felip Neri *(p84)*, with its picturesque church and simple stone fountain, provides a beautiful set piece for a photo.

5 Park Güell
Gaudí's fairy-tale imagination was let loose on this spectacular park *(p32)*. The colourfully tiled salamander at the entrance staircase and the stunning panorama from the sinuous bench on the main square are the classic shots photographers seek, but both also offer postcard views. There are scores of other exquisite details that will catch every photographer's eye.

A sandy beach at the popular resort town of Sitges, near Barcelona

6 Castell de Montjuïc

This castle's bastions (p99) enjoy one of the best vantage points over the entire city offer incredible, panoramic views. The ramparts also enable you to place several landmarks in the same frame. For a photo of a different side to the city, take some shots of the multicoloured shipping containers in the port.

7 Museu d'Art Contemporani

Barcelona's contemporary art museum, MACBA (p42) is housed in a striking white building overlooking a huge, modern square. The square has become a hotspot for skateboarders, and their swift moves make for great action shots.

8 Bunkers del Carmel

Tucked away in a quiet suburb are the Bunkers del Carmel (p56), which date back to the Spanish Civil War (p11). Today the incredible panoramic views from here make this the perfect spot from which to photograph the city, particularly as the sun is setting. It's hardly surprising that these bunkers are now one of the city's most photographed viewpoints, so expect to find other budding photographers vying for that perfect shot.

The iconic rainbow-hued Ferris wheel at Tibidabo

9 Tibidabo Ferris Wheel

Catch a ride on the charming and historic Ferris wheel at the Tibidabo funfair (p119) to recreate a classic Barcelona shot: the pretty, rainbow-coloured cars juxtaposed against the sights of the city laid out at your feet.

10 Beaches

It's hard to get a bad picture of the beaches (p105) in Barcelona. A dawn shot of the tall, diaphanous sculpture, *The Wounded Star*, by Rebecca Horn on Barceloneta beach is always a winner. There are also many gorgeous spots just a short distance from the city, such as the beaches of Sitges (p129).

OUTDOOR BARS

1 El Jardí
The Gothic courtyard of a medieval hospital (*p93*) provides a beautiful backdrop to this outdoor café, which is a quiet oasis in the heart of El Raval. The tables are arranged around a pretty garden, strung with fairy lights. It's a great spot for winding down with a cocktail after a day of sightseeing.

2 Antic Teatre Café-Bar
Tucked away in a minuscule alley, this leafy outdoor bar (*p87*) is attached to a theatre and is a popular meeting place for actors and musicians. Perfect for a quiet coffee during the day, the bar has a relaxed atmosphere. Once night falls, it is transformed into a magical secret garden. Sit on the terrace or in the garden, and enjoy a glass of wine.

3 Bar Kasparo
This laid-back outdoor bar (*p96*) serves a varied menu of fresh international fare made with a modern twist. Must-try dishes here include chicken curry and Greek salad. With outdoor seating in a quiet, traffic-free square, this bar is great for whiling away time. By day this is a popular spot with families, thanks to the play area it overlooks, but after the sun dips beneath the horizon a bar-like vibe takes hold of the place, fuelled by beer and cider.

4 Bar Calders
Carrer del Parlament is packed with plenty of trendy boutiques and restaurants, but Bar Calders (*p103*) stands out for its charming terrace, tasty tapas and delightful staff. Visit the bar and you'll see why it's one of the best places in the city for a *vermut* (vermouth) with an accompanying dish of olives.

5 La Caseta del Migdia
Situated in the pine forest behind Montjuïc Castle, this is a summer-only bar (*p103*). Fabulous views, ice-cold beers and the occasional live jazz concert or DJ session make this an irresistible spot to escape the heat on summer nights and watch the sunset.

Gorgeous terrace of La Caseta del Migdia

6 Torre Rosa

Located in the courtyard of a pink-hued centenary villa, this bar *(p124)* provides the perfect summer retreat, away from the hustle and bustle of the city. Come here to enjoy expertly mixed cocktails under the cool shade of palm trees – as the locals do.

7 Cotton House Hotel Terrace

Housed in a listed landmark building, now a luxury hotel, this enormous terrace bar *(p115)* is furnished with plush chairs and sofas that are shaded by numerous luxuriant plants. It's a fashionable address to enjoy wines, excellent cocktails and upmarket tapas.

8 Jardín del Alma

It's hard to believe that you are in the middle of a metropolitan city once you step into this beautiful and deeply romantic garden retreat, part of the elegant Alma Barcelona Hotel. People come here from all over for fine wines, cocktails, and quite a few exquisite tapas, but stay for the good vibes .

9 Fragments Cafè

A friendly local café located in one of the loveliest squares in the city, Fragments Café *(p125)* is not the place to eat in a hurry. Take your time and enjoy your meal in the pretty, plant-filled garden at the back, where you can dine by candlelight on balmy summer evenings.

10 Bus Terraza

A London double-decker bus pulled up by the seafront *(p108)* has become one of Barcelona's hottest garden terraces – and there's nearly always a queue to get in. Sink into one of the deckchairs or loungers, and enjoy DJ sets and live music with your cocktail.

The DJ booth at Bus Terraza, a rooftop bar in the Parc del Fòrum

TAPAS DISHES

Coloured sausages hanging in La Boqueria Market

1 Fuet

Catalonia is famous throughout Spain for its *embotits*, an umbrella term for a range of cured sausages, the most common of which is *fuet*. A dry-cured sausage made with pork and seasoned with garlic and black pepper, it's usually served in thin slices. Pair it with a perfectly poured cold beer at El Vaso de Oro (*p107*).

2 Patates Braves

One of the most famous Spanish tapas dishes, *patates braves* are delectable chunks of fried potatoes topped with a spicy sauce. There is considerable debate about what constitutes the most authentic *brava* (spicy) sauce: the classic gets its colour and flavour from smoked paprika but many bars add a dollop of mayonnaise or aioli and use a tomato-based sauce.

3 Pa amb tomàquet

This Catalan classic is one of those simple dishes that's more than the sum of its parts. It's just a slice of rustic bread, sometimes toasted, rubbed with fresh tomato, perhaps garlic, then drizzled with olive oil and a sprinkling of salt. Some places offer a "make your own" plate, with bread, tomato and garlic.

4 Croquetes

Typically, *croquetes* are made with bechamel sauce and a filling, usually cod, ham, chicken or spinach, then coated in breadcrumbs and fried, to create a crusty coat that contrasts with the unctuous filling. Contemporary chefs are throwing out tradition in favour of more unusual fillings such as prawn, squid ink or wild mushroom. Sample such fillings at Bar del Pla (*p88*).

5 Musclos

Mussels appear regularly on Catalan menus and are usually served *al vapor* (steamed), *a la marinera* (in white wine or parsley), a *l'all* (with garlic) or *a la crema* (with a cream sauce). Seek out restaurants serving mussels from the Delta de l'Ebre, the beautiful wetlands in the south of the region, to try the best in Catalunya.

6 Bombas

Incredibly filling, *bombas* are tasty balls of mashed potato with a slightly spicy meaty filling, which are coated in breadcrumbs, fried and then topped with aioli and a spicy tomato sauce. They are particularly popular in the old fishing neighbourhood of Barceloneta.

7 Truita de Patates

Prepared with sliced, boiled potato and fried onions and eggs, and served in tapas bars across the city, this thick

A table filled with numerous popular tapas dishes

potato omelette is a local favourite. Visitors should sample it with some alternative fillings such as *carbassó* (courgette), *alberginia* (aubergine) or *carxofa* (artichoke), all of which are delicious. For the best range of *truita*, head to Cervecería Catalana (*p117*).

8 Escalivada
This is a pure Catalan dish – the stripes in the dish are said to represent the Catalan flag. It consists of roast or grilled peppers, aubergine and onions served cold or slightly warmed, and is a popular topping on *coca* (a flatbread). You'll find the best at El Quim de la Boqueria (*p97*) in La Boqueria market.

9 Pernil Serrà
Serrano ham (which is cured, rather than cooked) is a hugely popular dish throughout Spain, and especially in Catalonia. It's the most common kind of ham, but there are different levels of quality, depending on the time it has been aged. Seek out these different serranos at restaurants across the city or hit the shops to buy some for yourself.

10 Calamars
Squid is a key part of tapas and restaurants generally serve it either *a la romana* (battered and fried) or *farcits* (stuffed) with prawns or meat. It's also a key part of the classic Mediterranean rice dish, *arròs negre* (black rice), which is similar to paella but cooked with squid ink. Cal Pep (*p89*) has some of the best in the city.

TOP 10
CAFÉ DRINKS

1. Cigaló
For coffee with a bite, try a *cigaló* (*carajillo*), which has a shot of either *conyac* (cognac), whisky or *ron* (rum).

2. Tallat and Café Sol
A *tallat* is a small cup of coffee with a dash of milk. A *cafè sol* is just plain coffee. In the summer, opt for either one *amb gel* (with ice).

3. Cafè amb llet
Traditionally enjoyed in the morning, *cafè amb llet* is a large milky coffee.

4. Orxata
This sweet, milky-white drink made from the tiger nut is a local summer time favourite.

5. Granissat
Slake your thirst with a cool *granissat*, a crushed-ice drink that is usually lemon-flavoured.

6. Aigua
Stay hydrated with *aigua mineral* (mineral water) – *amb gas* is sparkling, *sense gas*, still.

7. Cacaolat
A chocolate-milk concoction, which is one of Spain's most popular sweet drink exports.

8. Una Canya and Una Clara
Una canya is roughly a quarter litre of *cervesa de barril* (draught beer). *Una clara* is the same size but made up of equal parts beer and fizzy lemonade.

9. Cava
Catalonia's answer to champagne is its home-grown *cava* – Freixenet and Codorníu are the most famous brands.

10. Vermut
Fortified wine served with a spritz of soda water. Going out for the *vermutada* is a popular ritual for the locals.

A full glass of cava with a strawberry

SHOPPING DESTINATIONS

1 Passeig de Gràcia
📍 E3

Set in the heart of the city, Barcelona's grand avenue of lavish Modernista buildings is fittingly home to some of the city's premier fashion and design stores. From the international big league (Chanel, Gucci, Dior, Stella McCartney) to Spain's heavy hitters (Camper, Loewe, Zara, Bimba y Lola, Mango), it's all here. The wide boulevards on either side feature more designer shopping, notably the pedestrianized Carrer Consell de Cent, which is also dotted with many art galleries, and Carrers Mallorca, València and Roselló.

2 Carrer Girona
📍 P1

Those looking for fashion bargains should head to Carrer Girona (metro Tetuan), which is lined with designer and high-street outlet stores. Most of these offer women's fashions including streetwear from brands such as Mango, evening wear and shoes from Catalan designers Etxart & Panno, and upmarket designs from the likes of Javier Simorra.

3 Plaça de Catalunya and Carrer Pelai
📍 L1 & M1

The city's busy centre is also its commercial crossroads, flanked by the department store El Corte Inglés and the shopping mall El Triangle, which includes FNAC (books, music, electronic) and Séphora (perfumes and cosmetics). Nearby Carrer Pelai is said to be the busiest pedestrian shopping street in Spain, lined with enough shoe and fashion shops to take up a whole afternoon. A short stroll brings you to Carrer Tallers with lots of vintage and secondhand fashion stores.

Barcelona's main shopping street,
Passeig de Gràcia

4 Maremagnum
☑ E6 ☑ Muelle de España 5
🕐 10am–9pm daily

This shopping and entertainment
centre is located right on the water's
edge, and is open every day of the
year. All of the main clothing chains
can be found here, along with a good
variety of cafés and restaurants.

5 Portal de l'Àngel
☑ M2

Once a Roman thoroughfare leading
into the walled city of Barcino, today
the pedestrian street of Portal de
l'Àngel is traversed by hordes of
shoppers toting bulging bags. The
street is chock-full of shoe, clothing,
jewellery and accessory shops.

6 Rambla de Catalunya

The genteel, classier extension
of La Rambla, this well-maintained
street (p112) offers a refreshing change
from its cousin's more downmarket
carnival atmosphere. Chic shops and
cafés pepper the street's length from
Plaça de Catalunya to Diagonal. Here
you'll find everything from fine foot-
wear and leather bags to linens and
decorative lamps.

7 Carrer Portaferrissa
☑ M3

Offering an eclectic range of items,
including zebra platform shoes,
bellybutton rings and pastel baby
T-shirts, this street's other name
could well be Carrer "Trendy". In
addition to all the usual high-street
chains – from H&M to Mango to
NafNaf – along this strip you'll find
El Mercadillo, crammed with hip
little shops selling spiked belts,
frameless sunglasses, surf wear
and the like. After stocking up on
new fashion pieces, stop for a box
of prettily wrapped and very tasty
chocolates at Fargas on the nearby
Carrer del Pi (No. 16).

8 Gràcia
☑ F1

Old bookstores, family-run grocery
stores and independent boutiques
selling trendy, often vintage, fashion,
homewares and accessories cluster
along Carrer Astúries (and its side
streets) and along Travessera de
Gràcia. A string of contemporary
clothing and shoe shops also line
Gran de Gràcia.

9 El Born
☑ P4

Amid El Born's web of streets are
all sorts of art and design shops (p82).
Passeig del Born and Carrer Rec are
dotted with innovative little galleries
(from sculpture to interior design),
plus clothing and shoe boutiques.
This is the best area for original
fashion and accessories.

10 Avinguda Diagonal
☑ D1

The Avinguda Diagonal – a busy
avenue that cuts diagonally across
the entire city – is hard to miss. It is a
premier shopping street, with shops
running from the west of Passeig de
Gràcia to its culmination in L'Illa mall
and the huge El Corte Inglés department store close to Plaça Maria Cristina.
Lining this stretch is a host of high-end
clothing and shoe stores – including
Armani, Loewe and Hugo Boss – as well
as interior design shops, jewellery and
watch purveyors, and more.

**Browsing homeware at a store on
Avinguda Diagonal**

MARKETS

1 Book and Coin Market at Mercat de Sant Antoni

🚇 D2 🏛 C/Comte d'Urgell 🕐 8am–3pm Sun 🌐 mercatdominical desantantoni.com

For book lovers, there's no better way to spend Sunday morning than browsing at this market in Sant Antoni. You'll find a mind-boggling assortment of weathered paperbacks, ancient tomes, stacks of old magazines, comics, postcards and lots more.

2 Fira de Santa Llúcia

🚇 N3 🏛 Pl de la Seu 🕐 1–23 Dec: 10am–8pm daily (hours may vary)

The festive season is officially under way when local artisans set up shop outside the cathedral for the annual Christmas fair. Well worth a visit, if only to peruse the *caganers*, miniature figures squatting to *fer caca* (take a poop). Uniquely Catalan, the *caganers* are usually hidden away at the back of nativity scenes. This unusual celebration of the scatological also appears in other Christmas traditions.

3 Els Encants

Trading beneath metal canopies, Els Encants *(p112)* is one of Europe's oldest flea markets, dating back to the 14th century. It sells everything from second-hand clothes and toys to electrical appliances and used books. Discerning shoppers can fit out an entire kitchen from the array of pots and pans available. Bargain-hunters should come early.

4 Mercat de la Boqueria

The most famous food market in Barcelona is conveniently located on La Rambla *(p26)*. Freshness reigns supreme and shoppers are spoiled for choice, with hundreds of stalls selling everything from vine-ripened tomatoes and haunches of beef to aromatic seafood and wedges of Manchego cheese. Be sure to stop by one of the atmospheric counter bars here, ideal for a quick lunch stop or a coffee break.

5 Mercat de Barceloneta

🚇 F6 🏛 Pl Font 1, Barceloneta 🕐 7am–3pm Mon–Thu & Sat, 7am–8pm Fri 🌐 mercatdela barceloneta.com

The striking Barceloneta market overlooks an expansive square. In addition to lively produce stalls, there is a good selection of bars and bakeries with fresh products to try.

Vintage clocks, gramophones and more at the Mercat dels Antiquaris

6 Mercat dels Antiquaris

🚇 N3 🏛 Pl de la Seu 🕐 10am–8pm Thu 🚫 Aug) 🌐 mercatgoticbcn.com

Antiques aficionados and collectors contentedly rummage through vintage jewellery, watches, embroidery and bric-a-brac at this long-running antiques market in front of the cathedral.

7 Fira de Filatelia i Numismàtica

🚇 L4 🏛 Pl Reial 🕐 9am–2:30pm Sun

Arranged around the elegant Plaça Reial (p82), this stamp and coin market draws avid collectors from across town. The newest collectors' items are phone cards and old *xapes de cava* (*cava* bottle cork foils). When the market ends –and the local police go to lunch – a makeshift flea market takes over. Old folks and immigrants from the *barri* haul out their antique wares – old lamps, clothing, junk – and lay it out for sale on the ground.

8 Fira Artesana

🚇 L3 🏛 Pl del Pi 🕐 10am– 10pm 1st & 3rd Fri, Sat & Sun of the month

The Plaça del Pi (p53) brims with natural and organic foods during the Fira Artesana, when artisanal food producers bring their goods to this

Stalls at the vast Els Encants, one of Barcelona's busiest flea markets

corner of the Barri Gòtic. The market specializes in homemade cheeses and honey – from clear clover honey from the Pyrenees to nutty concoctions from Reus.

9 Mercat del Art de la Plaça de Sant Josep Oriol

🚇 M3 🏛 Pl de Sant Josep Oriol 🕐 11am–8:30pm Sat, 10am–3pm Sun

At weekends, local artists flock to this Barri Gòtic square (p80) to set up their easels and sell their art. You'll find a range including watercolours of Catalan landscapes and oil paintings of churches and castles.

10 Mercat de Santa Caterina

🚇 N3 🏛 Av Francesc Cambó 16 🕐 7:30am–3:30pm Mon, Wed & Sat, 7:30am–8:30pm Tue, Thu & Fri 🌐 mercatsanta caterina.com

Each *barri* has its own food market with tempting displays but this one has a truly spectacular setting to pair with the food. It is housed in an eye-catching, colourful building, which was one of the final buildings designed by the renowned Catalan architect Enric Miralles (1955–2000).

BARCELONA FOR FREE

1 Open House Barcelona
🖥 48hopenhousebarcelona.org
Peek into private homes and historic
monuments during Barcelona's
annual Open House weekend. Many
buildings not usually open to the
public can be explored, including
the Arc de Triomf and the Ateneu
cultural centre.

2 Sunday Afternoons at City Museums
All city-run museums offer free
admission at least one afternoon a
month, usually the first Saturday or
Sunday of the month, and several,
including the Museu de Catalunya,
Museu del Disseny, Centre de Cultura
Contemporánea de Barcelona (CCCB),
Museu de la Història de Barcelona
(MUHBA) and Museu Blau (main site
of the Museu de Ciències Naturals),
are free Sunday afternoon from 3pm.
A full list of these can be found on
the Barcelona Turisme website *(bar
celonaturisme.com/wv3/en/enjoy/25/
a-zero-cost-cultural-afternoon.html)*.

3 Font Màgica
The Magic Fountain *(p99)* thrills
with its sound and light shows – in
which multicoloured jets of water leap
to different soundtracks in elegant
rows all the way up to the MNAC on the
hill behind. The programme, ranging
from classical to Disney tunes, is on
the Barcelona Turisme website. Festes
de la Mercè's closing event, the
Piromusical (a fireworks and laser
show), also takes place here.

4 Festes
Every neighbourhood has its
own *festa major* (various dates, Jun–
Sep), ranging from the bacchanalian
romp in Gràcia to the more modest
celebrations of Poble Sec. One of
the biggest festivals is the Festes
de la Mercè. You will see various
Catalan traditions, from *castells*

A fireworks display during the Festes de la Mercè

(human towers) to *correfocs*
(fire-running) – and all for free.

5 La Capella
📍 K3 🏛 C/Hospital 56 🕐 Hours
vary, check website 🖥 lacapella.
barcelona
The chapel at the Antic Hospital de
la Santa Creu *(p94)* has been converted into a fantastic art space
hosting exhibitions of contemporary
works by up-and-coming artists.

6 Cinema Lliure al Platja
📍 E6 🖥 cinemalliure.com/platja
Platja beach hosts free screenings of
independent films during the summer
months. One evening a week (usually
Thursdays) during July and August,
locals settle down on beach towels at
sunset to enjoy a movie. Sometimes
there's live music too. Check out the
website for the summer schedule.

7 Spectacular Panoramas
With its wealth of *miradors*
(viewpoints), Barcelona offers ample
opportunity to contemplate the city's
beauty. Relax over a glass of fizzing
cava at Bunkers del Carmel *(p56)* and

atch the dazzling lights as the sun
ets. Or head up to Mount Tibidabo,
etter known as "the magic mountain",
hich is equally popular for its views.

Carretera de les Aigües

Running along the side of the
ollserola park (p121), this path is
opular with mountain-bikers and
unners, and offers spectacular views
cross the city and out to sea. Getting
ere is fun too: take the FGC train
 Peu de la Funicular, then ride the
unicular up to the *carretera* stop.

Street Art

The streets are filled with art by
orld-renowned artists including
otero's *Cat* on the Rambla del Raval;
ichtenstein's *Head of Barcelona* and
ariscal's *Gambrinus* at the city port;
ehry's glittering *Fish* by the sea; and
iró's *Woman and Bird* in the Parc de
an Miró (p55) and mosaic at the
ercat de la Boqueria (p26).

Beaches

Barcelona has ten beaches, which
ollectively stretch for over 4.5 km (3
iles) along the coast. There are also
cenic beach towns like Sitges nearby.
etween Easter and October these are
otted with *xiringuitos* selling drinks and
nacks, and have lifeguards, sun lounger
ental and even a beach library.

**he beautiful resort town of Sitges,
nown for its golden sandy beaches**

TOP 10
BUDGET TIPS

1. Pack a picnic of delicious local
produce and head to the Montjuïc
parks (the Parc Jacint Mossen Cinto
with its lily ponds and shady nooks
is a particular favourite) or to the
beaches to dine for a fraction of
the price of a restaurant.

2. If you are going to be visiting a
lot of museums and using the public transport system, invest in the
Barcelona Card, which starts at €53
for 72 hours (10 per cent discount
on online bookings).

3. The Art Ticket, which provides
entry to six major art museums
for €38, is an excellent deal for
culture buffs.

4. Download the Too Good to Go
app, which lists surplus food sold
at reduced prices by restaurants
and bakeries.

5. Several theatres and cinemas offer
reduced prices on *Dia del Espectador*,
usually on Monday, Tuesday or
Wednesday, or for the day's first
performance (usually around 4pm).

6. At weekday lunchtimes, many
restaurants serve a good-value
menú del migdia with two or three
courses, a glass of wine and perhaps a coffee.

7. The best travel option is
the T-Casual, a travel card valid
for ten journeys in zones 1 to 6
and the airport train (not for the
airport metro).

8. Some university residences,
such as the Residència Àgora BCN
and the Residència Erasmus, offer
cheap beds during the summer break.

9. For fashion bargains, hit the
outlet stores on Carrer Girona, near
the Gran Via. Brands include Mango,
Etxart & Panno and Nice Things.

10. All of the products offered by
Barcelona's tourist service, from the
Bus Turístic to walking tours, are sold
at a discount (usually 10 per cent)
on its website.

FESTIVALS AND EVENTS

1 Colourful Carnivals

Barcelona's week-long carnival season kicks off on Dijous Gras (last Thursday before Lent) with a parade up the Rambla. Led by the carnival king and queen, it culminates in a confetti battle. The beach town of Sitges (p129) has the biggest celebration, with over-the-top floats carrying performers.

2 Llum BCN

In February, Barcelona's festival of light transforms the revitalized former warehouse district of Poblenou. The buildings, galleries and squares flicker with light sculptures, installations and shows in a stunning display.

3 El Dia de Sant Jordi

On 23 April, the day of Sant Jordi (p47), Barcelonans exchange books and roses, sold at stalls across the city. The rose petals symbolize the blood of the slain dragon, while the books are a tribute to Cervantes and Shakespeare, who both died on 23 April 1616.

4 Castells

The tradition of building *castells* (human towers) in Catalonia dates back to the 18th century. In June, trained *castellers* stand on each other's shoulders to create a human castle – the highest tower takes the prize. *Castells* are often performed in Plaça Sant Jaume.

5 Summer Arrives

In celebration of St John and the start of summer, 23 June is Catalonian night to play with fire – and play they do, with gusto. Fireworks streak through the night sky and bonfires are set ablaze on beaches and in towns throughout the region.

6 LGBTQ+ Events

🌐 pridebarcelona.org; circuitfestival.net/Barcelona
Barcelona has a lively LGBTQ+ scene, with specialist bookshops, hip boutiques and chic clubs that pulsate into the early hours. In June, the city celebrates Pride with fabulous floats, concerts and a full programme of talks and activities. The Circuit Festival in August is a sizzling event, where people flock to Barcelona's beaches for a huge LGBTQ+ party.

7 Neighbourhood Festivals

Barcelona is a city that enjoys a party. During the summer months, every neighbourhood has some form of celebration. The best known *festa major* is in Gràcia in mid-August, famous for its extravagantly decorated streets and outdoor concerts. Other neighbourhood festivals include Poble Sec in July and Sants in August, both of which feature traditional parades and *correfocs* (fire-running).

correfoc **performance during the
Festes de la Mercè**

8 Festes de la Mercè
W barcelona.cat/lamerce
Barcelona's main festival is a riotous
week-long celebration in September in
honour of La Mercè, a co-patron saint
of the city *(p47)*. The night sky lights up
with fireworks, concerts are held and
there are parades of *gegants* and *capgrossos* (giants and fatheads). Don't
miss the *correfoc*, when fire-spitting
dragons career through the streets.

9 The Big Screen
W sitgesfilmfestival.com
Every October Barcelona hosts the
Sitges Film Festival, the world's biggest
celebration of fantasy and horror films.
Outdoor screenings are held during the
summer, with the *Gandules* (deckchairs)
festival featuring arthouse films.

10 Christmas Celebrations
The Nadal (Christmas) season
begins on 1 December with artisan fairs.
Fira de Santa Llúcia, Barcelona's oldest
Christmas market, sees stalls set up
around Catedral de Barcelona selling
handmade gifts. On 5 January is the
spectacular Cavalcada de Reis (Parade of
the Three Kings). The kings arrive by ship
into the city's harbour and then parade
through streets lined with children. In
Spain, the kings bring the children their
presents on this magical night.

Awe-inspiring *castells* being formed
during a festival in Catalonia

TOP 10
MUSIC, THEATRE
AND ART FESTIVALS

1. Guitar BCN
W guitarbcn.com
An international guitar festival
organized by Spanish music
promoters, The Project.

2. Jazz Terrassa
W jazzterrassa.org
This internationally renowned festival
offers jazz concerts in venues around
the town of Terrassa.

3. Ciutat Flamenco
W ciutatflamenco.com
A week of outstanding flamenco music
and dance at venues around the city.

4. Primavera Sound
W primaverasound.com
Many big names are featured in
this pop, rock and underground
dance music festival.

5. Festival del Sónar
W sonar.es
This festival is an explosion of
music and the latest in audio-
visual production.

6. Grec Festival Barcelona
W barcelona.cat/grec
Barcelona's largest music, theatre
and dance festival.

7. Crüilla
W cruillabarcelona.com
Huge summer festival in the Parc
del Fòrum, with big-name bands
and emerging talent.

8. Alma Festival
W almafestival.com
Held in the Poble Espanyol *(p101)*,
Alma hosts international rock and
pop acts.

9. Festival de Llums Antiga
W auditori.cat
A regular season of early music
held at the city's oldest and most
atmospheric churches.

**10. Festival Internacional de Jazz
de Barcelona**
W jazz.barcelona
Jazz festival with experimental music
and big-names, held all over the city.

SPORTS AND OUTDOOR ACTIVITIES

1 Football
There is no bigger institution in the city than FC Barça. Though the iconic Camp Nou stadium is under renovation, the site is still worth visiting for the Museu del FC Barcelona (p120) covering the club's history. Afterwards, catch a game at the club's temporary home, Estadi Lluís Companys, or see FC Barcelona Femení at Johan Cruyff Stadium.

2 Cycling
Barcelonans have enthusiastically embraced cycling, and the city now has more than 300 km (186 miles) of bike lanes. Rent a bike or take a tour run by Steel Donkey Bike Tours (steeldonkey biketours.com). If you prefer mountain-biking, the Parc de Collserola (p121) has scores of trails perfect for all levels.

3 Sailing
Thanks to the calm waters of the Mediterranean, the city is the perfect place for boating. Earn your captain's stripes with Base Nautica (basenautica.org) or take it easy and rent a yacht with a skipper through Barcelona Boat Tours (barcelonaboatours.com). Escape to the Cap de Creus marine reserve (p131) for some breathtakingly beautiful sailing.

4 Beach Volleyball
Amble along the beachfront and you'll see numerous nets set up for beach volleyball, a great way to soak up the sun. Most nets are found on the Nova Icària beach and best of all, they're free. Just get there early as they're on a first-come-first-served basis.

5 Hiking
There are several wonderful hiking trails in Barcelona with the best of the routes in the Parc de Collserola (p121). This park offers well-marked trails that are great for a family stroll or a strenuous hike. Serious hikers will enjoy the jagged peaks of Montserrat (p127) or the stunning coastal paths – known as the Camins de Ronda – that connect turquoise coves in the Costa Brava (p128).

6 Climbing
Barcelona is ideally located for climbers, with many challenging sites nearby and the Pyrenees to the north. Montserrat (p127) has excellent routes for solo climbers while guided climbs are offered by Climb In Catalunya (climbincatalunya.com). Within the city itself, Climbat (climbat.com), an indoor climbing centre on Montjuïc, has walls for all levels to practise on before.

7 Yoga
Barcelonans have fallen for wellness and today the city is chock-a-block with yoga studios offering every type

Stand-up paddleboarding in the Mediterranean se

FC Barcelona in action at the
Camp Nou stadium

of this popular activity from Ashtanga
to Vinyasa. Find your favourite class at
YogaOne (*yogaone.es*), which has 15
centres across the city. Or, for something
truly special, Ocean Breath (*oceanbreath
barcelona.com*) offers yoga on the
beach as you watch the sunrise.

8 Tennis and padel

The popularity of tennis has
grown thanks to the success of Spanish
players, who can be seen playing at the
Barcelona Open in April. Inspired? There
are plenty of tennis clubs to test your
own skills, or try the smaller courts used
for *padel*, a mix of tennis and squash,
with clubs located throughout the city.

9 Running

Barcelona doesn't lack for great
running routes, whether it's the beachfront promenade, the parks of Montjuïc
(*p98*) or the wooded paths around the
Park Güell. More adventurous runners
should take the tiny funicular to the
Carretera de las Aigües and tackle the
trail that winds along the Collserola
hillside with views of the city below.

10 Watersports

Watersports are hugely popular in
Barcelona and the seas off the city hold
a great range of aquatic activities from
stand-up paddleboarding (SUP) to kite
surfing. Beginners can wobble through
a SUP or surfing lesson with Sea You
(*seayoubarcelona.com*), while the more
advanced should take on the city's best
waves at Bogatell. Once you have your
sea legs, head to the Costa Brava for
guided kayaking trips with Kayaking
Costa Brava (*kayakingcostabrava.com*).

TOP 10
CATALAN SPORTS PERSONALITIES

1. Alexia Putellas
Captain of Spain's women's football
team and FC Barcelona Femení,
Putellas is considered one of the
greatest players of all time.

2. Pep Guardiola
Regarded as one of the greatest
football managers of all time,
Guardiola has both played for
and managed FC Barça.

3. Carlos Puyol
"The shark" was a stalwart for
Barça, playing in defence between
1999–2014 and captaining the club
for ten of those years.

4. Gerard Piqué
Piqué was a legendary player for both
Barça and Spain, and was the bedrock
of the defence alongside Carlos Puyol.

5. Xavi Hernández
Hernández playmaking prowess
earned him a place in the Ballon d'Or
Dream Team, as well as World Cup and
European Championship triumphs.

6. Marc Márquez
An eight-time World Champion,
Marquez is the most successful
Spanish motorcycle racer.

7. Alex Palou
A two-time IndyCar Series Champion,
Palou is the first Spanish driver to win
an open-wheel national championship in the USA.

8. Pau Gasol
Along with his brother, Marc, Pau
Gasol is one of the most celebrated
basketball players in the NBA and has
also represented Spain in the Olympics.

9. Mireia Belmonte
Belmonte is one of Spain's greatest-
ever swimmers, with numerous
Olympic gold medals and world
championship titles.

10. Laia Sana
A trailblazer in off-road racing, Sana
boasts multiple Dakar Rally victories
and has represented Spain in the
International Six Days Enduro (ISDE).

AREA BY AREA

Barcelona Cathedra

BARRI GÒTIC AND LA RIBERA

Starting as the Roman settlement of Barcino, the city grew over the years, with a building boom taking place in the 14th and 15th centuries. Barri Gòtic, a beautifully pre-served neighbourhood of Gothic buildings, lively squares and atmospheric alleys, exemplifies the area's medieval heyday. Extending east of Barri Gòtic is the ancient La Ribera, a neighbourhood that has been the commercial and artisanal heart of Barcelona since the Middle Ages.

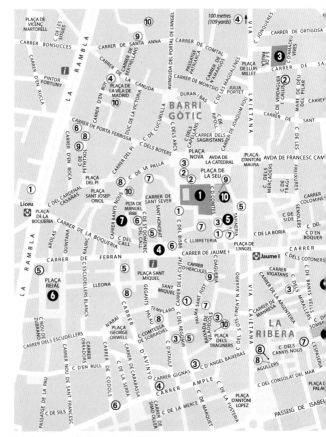

For places to stay in this area, see p144

The Palau de la Generalitat on Plaça de Sant Jaume

1 Barcelona Cathedral

Soaring over the Barri Gòtic is Barcelona's mighty cathedral *(p28)*, which dates from 1298.

2 Museu Picasso

Discover the youthful output *(p38)* of one of the most revered artists of the 20th century. The pieces on display here range from Picasso's precocious sketches and family portraits to his Blue- and Rose-period works.

3 Palau de la Música Catalana

The city's most prestigious concert hall *(p40)* is a breathtaking monument to both *la música* Catalana and the Modernista aesthetic.

4 Plaça de Sant Jaume

🅚 M4 🅓 Palau de la Generalitat: 012 🅓 For guided tours, chech website for details; Ajuntament: 10am–1:30pm Sun for guided tours (English at 10am)
🆆 presidencia.gencat.cat 🅓

The site at which the Plaça de Sant Jaume lies today was once the nucleus of Roman Barcino. With these roots, it seems fitting that the square is home to Barcelona's two most important government buildings – the Palau de la Generalitat (the seat of Catalonian parliament) and the Ajuntament (city hall). Look out for the detailed carved relief of Sant Jordi, Catalonia's patron saint, on the 15th-century Generalitat façade. Within is the beautiful 1434 Capella de Sant Jordi *(p47)*. A highlight of the Gothic 15th-century Ajuntament is the Saló de Cent, from where the Council of One Hundred, Barcelona's first form of government, ruled from 1372 to 1714. Also worth exploring is the Pati dels Tarongers, a lovely arcaded courtyard planted with orange trees and overlooked by interesting gargoyles.

Three Graces fountain in the centre of Plaça Reial

5 Museu d'Història de Barcelona (MUHBA)

⬡ N4 ⬡ Pl del Rei ⬡ 10am–7pm Tue–Sun (to 8pm Sun) ⬡ barce lona.cat/museuhistoria ⬡

The medieval Plaça del Rei (p52) contains the core site of the excellent Museu d'Història de Barcelona, encompassing remains ranging from Roman Barcino to the Middle Ages. These include Casa Padellàs and the Palau Reial, which contains the Capella de Santa Àgata (p47) and the Saló del Tinell, a massive arched hall where the royal monarchs of the newly united Spain, Ferdinand and Isabel. met Columbus after his 1492 voyage to the Americas. The museum also has one of the largest under-ground excavations of Roman ruins on display in Europe (p85), including a 3rd-century garum factory and winery.

6 Plaça Reial

⬡ L4

Late 19th-century elegance meets sangria-drinking café society in the arcaded Plaça Reial, one of the city's most entertaining squares. The Modernista lampposts were designed by Gaudí in 1879, and at its centre is a wrought-iron fountain representing the *Three Graces*. The palm-lined square has a cluster of restaurants, bars and cafés that are constantly packed with locals.

7 El Call

⬡ M4

Derived from the Hebrew word *kahal*, meaning community or congregation, El Call was home to one of Spain's largest Jewish communities until their expulsion in the 15th century. Remnants of the medieval character of the area remains, even though few of the original buildings have survived. A small 5th-century synagogue (now restored) on Carrer de Marlet is believed to be one of the oldest in Europe. There is also an interpretation centre dedicated to El Call, run by the city's history museum and ancient Jewish baths in the basement of the Café Caelum.

8 Basílica de Santa Maria del Mar

⬡ P5 ⬡ Pl de Santa Maria 1 ⬡ 10am–8:30pm daily; cultural visit: 10am–6pm Mon–Sat, 1:30–5:30pm Sun ⬡ santamariadel marbarcelona.org ⬡ ⬡

The spacious, breathtaking interior of this 14th-century church, designed by the famous architect Berenguer de Montagut, is a premier example of the austere Catalan Gothic style. The church is dedicated to St Mary of the Sea, the patron saint of sailors, and an ancient model ship hangs near one of the statues of the Virgin. Dubbed "the people's church", this is a popular spot for exchanging wedding

---

EL BORN

If you're in the mood for a proper martini or some alternative jazz, then look no further than El Born, a medieval neighbourhood that's been "reborn" over the previous few decades. Students and artists moved in, attracted by cheap rents and airy spaces, fostering an arty vibe that now blends in with the area's old-time aura. Passeig de Born, lined with bars and cafés, leads onto Plaça Comercial, where the Born Market (in operation 1870–1970) has been converted into a cultural centre and exhibition space.

rows. The rooftop, accessed via the
bell towers, offers spectacular views
over the city.

9 Museu Etnològic i de Cultures del Món

P4 C/Montcada 14 10am–
8:30pm daily barcelona.cat/
museu-etnologic-culturesmon

The Museum of World Cultures, in
the 16th-century Nadal and Marqués
de Lió palaces, showcases the cultures
of Asia, Africa, America and Oceania.
Highlights include Hindu sculptures,
Japanese paintings, Nazca ceramics,
brass plaques from Benin and
indigenous Australian art.

10 Museu Frederic Marès

N3 Pl de Sant Iu 5–6
10am–7pm Tue–Sat, 11am–
8pm Sun barcelona.cat/
museufredericmares

This fascinating museum houses
the collection of Catalan sculptor
Frederic Marès. No mere hobby
collector, the astute (and obsessive)
Marès amassed holdings that a
modern museum curator would
die for. Among them are religious
icons and statues, dating from
Roman times to the present, and
the curious "Museu Sentimental",
which displays everything from
ancient watches to fans and dolls.
Also worth a visit during summer
is Cafè d'Estiu, a sunny spot on the
museum's patio.

A collection of ancient sculptures at
the Museu Frederic Marès

A STROLL THROUGH ROMAN BARCELONA

Morning

Start at the Jaume I metro stop.
Walk up Via Laietana to the **Plaça
de Ramon Berenguer el Gran**
(p84), which is backed by Roman
walls. Return to the metro and
turn right onto C/Jaume I to get to
the **Plaça de Sant Jaume,** the site
of the old Roman forum. Leading
off to the left is C/Ciutat, which
becomes C/Regomir: at No. 3 is
Pati Llimona, with an extensive
section of Roman walls, one of the
four gateways into the city and
the ruins of some thermal baths.
There's a good café at Pati
Llimona and the **Bodega La
Palma** (p89) serves tasty tapas.

Afternoon

Return to the Plaça de Sant
Jaume and cross it into C/Paradís,
to reach the **Temple d'August,** a
MUHBA site. At the end of the
street, turn right and make for the
Plaça del Rei (p52). Stop for coffee
at the **Café-Bar L'Antiquari** (p89)
before visiting the **Museu
d'Història de Barcelona** to explore
the Roman Barcino. Walk back to
C/Comtes, which flanks **Barcelona
Cathedral** (p28), turn right and
cross Plaça Nova to C/Arcs, which
leads to Avinguda Portal de
l'Àngel. Turn left down C/Canuda
to reach the **Plaça de la Vila de
Madrid** (p53), where you can find
several Roman sarcophagi.

The Best of the Rest

Neo-Gothic El Pont del Bisbe, maybe the city's most famous bridge

1. Carrer del Bisbe
M3

Medieval Carrer del Bisbe is flanked by the Gothic Cases dels Canonges (House of Canons) and the Palau de la Generalitat (p81). Connecting the two is a gorgeous 1928 arched stone bridge.

2. Carrer de Santa Llúcia
M3

This medieval street is home to the Casa de l'Ardiaca (p28), which features a patio, palm trees and a fountain.

3. Capella de Sant Cristòfol
M4 **C/Regomir 6–8**

Dedicated to Sant Cristòfor, the patron saint of travellers, this quaint chapel dates back to 1503, although it was remodelled in the 1890s. Drivers bring their cars to the chapel annually on the saint's feast day (25 July) to be blessed.

4. Carrer Montcada
P4

The "palace row" of La Ribera is lined with Gothic gems, including the 15th-century Palau Aguilar, now home to the Museu Picasso (p38), and the 17th-century Palau Dalmases with its chapel, which hosts flamenco performances.

5. Plaça de Ramon Berenguer el Gran
N3

This square is home to one of the largest preserved sections of Barcelona's impressive Roman walls.

6. Moco
P4 **C/Montcada 25** **10am–8pm daily (to 9pm Fri–Sun)** **mocomuseum.com**

Set in a medieval palace, Moco has a small but powerful collection of contemporary and street art. Featured artists include Yayoi Kusama, Banksy, Damien Hurst, Andy Warhol and Basquiat.

7. Plaça de Sant Felip Neri
M3

Sunlight filters through tall trees in this hidden oasis of calm. The square is home to an 18th-century church pocked by bomb damage from the Civil War.

8. Carrer Petritxol
L3

A beautiful, historic street, Carrer Petritxol is lined with *granges* and *xocolateries* (cafés and chocolate shops). The famous Sala Parés art gallery, which once exhibited Picasso, Casas and other Catalan artists, is also located here.

9. Basílica de Sant Just i Sant Pastor
M4 **Pl de Sant Just s/n** **basilicasantjust.cat**

This Gothic church, completed in 1342, has sculptures dating back to the 9th century and Visigothic baptismal fonts from the 5th century.

10. Església de Santa Anna
M2 **C/Santa Anna 29** **93 301 35 76**

Mere paces from La Rambla is this tranquil Romanesque church with a leafy 15th-century Gothic cloister.

Remains of Roman Barcino

1. MUHBA

Spread beneath MUHBA *(p82)* are the extensive remains of Barcino, the Roman settlement that grew into Barcelona. Some sections are remarkably intact, including roads still indented with cart ruts and laundry vats still stained with dye.

2. City Entrance Gate

⊙ M3 ⬚ Plaça Nova & Carrer del Bisbe

Towers flanking the entrance to Carrer del Bisbe are the remnants of the only surviving entrance gate to the Roman city, the 4th-century Porta Praetoria.

3. Aqueduct

⊙ M3 ⬚ Plaça Nova & Carrer del Bisbe

Opposite the Porta Praetoria is an archway, which was part of a reconstructed aqueduct. The aqueduct would have been one of several that brought water into the city. In front of it is Joan Brossa's visual poem *Barcino*.

4. Via Sepulcral Romana

⊙ M2 ⬚ Plaça Vila de Madrid ⬚ 11am–2pm Tue, 11am–3pm & 4–7pm Sun ⬚ barcelona.cat/museuhistoria ⬚

The Romans buried their dead in tombs outside the city walls. Several sarcophagi survive in this necropolis, which dates back to the 1st century, and are visible from the walkway spanning the Plaça Vila de Madrid.

5. Portal del Mar and Baths

⊙ M4 ⬚ C/Regomir, 7-9 ⬚ hours vary, check website ⬚ barcelona.cat/museuhistoria/la-porta-de-mar-i-les-termes-portuaries

Travellers and goods brought by ship would enter the city through this gate. A bath was obligatory for these travellers and the remnants of the baths can still be seen next to the gate.

6. Forum

⊙ M4 ⬚ Plaça Sant Jaume

This square was the forum and meeting point of the Roman settlement's main arteries: the *cardus* and the *decumanus*.

7. Temple d'August

⊙ M4 ⬚ C/Paradís s/n ⬚ barcelona.cat/museuhistoria

An alley just off the Plaça Sant Jaume leads to a quartet of 9-m- (30-ft-) high columns, the only remains of the Temple of Augustus from 1st century BCE.

8. Roman Domus

⊙ M4 ⬚ C/Avinyó 15 ⬚ 10am–2pm Sun ⬚ barcelona.cat/museuhistoria ⬚

This Roman house dates from the 1st–4th centuries and was discovered in 2004. Parts of the original wall paintings and mosaics can still be seen.

9. Walls and Moat

⊙ N3 ⬚ Plaça de Ramón Berenguer el Gran

One of the best-preserved sections of the Roman walls is studded with towers, which have been incorporated into the Plaça de Ramon Berenguer el Gran *(p84)*.

10. Defence Towers

⊙ E5 ⬚ Plaça Traginers

Dating back to the 4th century, this tall, circular watchtower is one of the 78 defensive constructions that were once part of the Roman walls.

Raised sarcophagi at the necropolis on Via Sepulcral Romana

Shops

1. Escribà Confiteria i Fleca
📍 L3 🏠 La Rambla 83 🌐 escriba.es

If the glistening pastries and towering chocolate creations aren't enough of a lure, then the Modernista storefront certainly is. Buy goodies to go or enjoy them in the café.

2. La Manual Alpargatera
📍 M4 🏠 C/Avinyó 7 🕐 Sun
🌐 lamanual.com

Notable personalities, including Pope John Paul II, Jack Nicholson and Salvador Dalí, have shopped for *alpargatas* (slip-on shoes or sandals) and espadrilles at this famous store.

3. Colmado
📍 P5 🏠 C/Brosoli 5
🌐 colmadoshop.com

This small boutique has a carefully curated selection of clothing and accessories from stylish labels such as Costa, Heinui and Wolf & Moon.

4. Sombreria Mil
📍 N1 🏠 C/Fontanella 20
🕐 Sun 🌐 sombreriamil.com

This century-old hat shop offers a fine range of headwear (including the traditional Catalan beret).

Handmade candles at the iconic Cereria Subirà

5. Beatriz Furest
📍 P5 🏠 C/Esparteria 1
🕐 Sun 🌐 beatrizfurest.com

Handcrafted bags and purses by Barcelonian designer Beatriz Furest are sold in this small, chic boutique.

6. Casa Colomina
📍 M3 🏠 C/Cucurulla 2 🌐 casa colomina.es

Sink your teeth into the Spanish nougat-and-almond speciality *torró*. Casa Colomina, established in 1908, offers a tantalizing array, including chocolate and marzipan varieties.

7. Cereria Subirà
📍 N4 🏠 Baixada Llibreteria 7
🕐 Sun 🌐 cereriasubira.cat

Founded in 1761, this is the city's oldest shop. It's crammed with every kind of candle imaginable.

8. Vila Viniteca
📍 N5 🏠 C/Agullers 7 🕐 Sun
🌐 vilaviniteca.es

This is one of the city's best wine merchants, stocking a wide range of wines and spirits. An adjoining shop sells quality Spanish delicacies, including hams, cheeses and olive oil.

9. Guantería Alonso
📍 M2 🏠 C/Santa Anna 27 🕐 Sun
🌐 guanteria-alonso.com

The long-established Guantería Alons is the place to visit for hand-painted fans, handmade gloves, mantillas and other traditional Spanish accessories.

10. L'Arca
📍 M3 🏠 C/Banys Nous 20
🌐 larcabarcelona.com

Find antique clothing, from flapper dresses to boned corsets, silk shawls, puff-sleeved shirts and wedding dresses here.

Vintage film posters and memorabilia at the 1980s-style Polaroid bar

Cocktail and Conversation Spots

1. Bar L'Ascensor
M4 C/Bellafila 3 **93 318 53 47**
6:30pm–1am daily
An old-fashioned, dark-wood elevator serves as the entrance to this dimly lit, convivial bar popular with a cocktail-swilling crowd.

2. Antic Teatre
N2 C/Verdaguer i Callís 12
11am–11pm Mon–Fri (to midnight Thu & Fri), 5pm–midnight Sat & Sun (to 11pm Sun) anticteatre.com
This café-bar is set in the courtyard of a small theatre. Take a seat at one of the tables, shaded by trees, for coffee or drinks.

3. Milk
M5 C/Gignàs 21 Hours vary, chech website milkbarcelona.com
Decorated like a luxurious living room, Milk serves a lovely brunch (from 9am to 4:30pm), lunch and dinner daily.

4. Las Cuevas de los Rajahs
E5 C/d' en Cignas 2 7pm–1am Wed–Sat lascuevas bar.com
With Neo-Gothic paraphernalia, this bar is set in a cave-like space and offers cocktails, beers and wine.

5. Glaciar
L4 Pl Reial 3 **93 302 11 63**
10am–2am daily
A café-bar, Glaciar is sought out for the front-row view of the *plaça* from its terrace.

6. Polaroid
M5 C/Còdols 29 7pm–2:30am daily polaroidbar.es
A bar with 80s-style decor and retro music, Polaroid offers well-priced drinks that come with free popcorn. Try to arrive early as this place is always packed.

7. La Vinya del Senyor
N5 Pl Santa Maria 5 Hours vary, chech website lavinyadel-senyor.es
Wine lovers from all over the city come here to sample a rich array of Spanish and international varieties.

8. Collage Art & Cocktail Social Club
N5 C/Consellers 4 7pm–2:30am Mon–Sat collagecochtailbar.com
Enjoy well-priced original cocktails at this spot. The lounge upstairs hosts exhibitions of pocket-size paintings.

9. Paradiso
F5 C/de Riera Palau 4 7am–2:30am daily paradiso.cat
This cocktail den is accessed speakeasy-style (you need to ask to be let in) via a gourmet sandwich bar. The drinks are artistically presented.

10. Mudanzas
P5 C/Vidrieria 15 **933 19 11 37**
6pm–2am daily (to 3am Fri & Sat)
With black-and-white tiled floors, and circular marble tables, Mudanzas has a fun, laid-back vibe.

Cafés and Light Eats

1. Mescladís
📍 P3 🏠 C/Carders 35 🌐 mes
cladis.org
This terrace café is run by an NGO that
provides culinary training to immigrants. Coffee, drinks and snacks
make for an ideal refreshment.

2. Demasié
📍 P4 🏠 C/de la Princesa 28
🌐 cookiesdemasie.com
Fresh juices, cold-pressed coffee, and
delicious cakes and cookies make this
bright-yellow establishment the perfect
place for a stopover. Take a seat on one
of their benches and enjoy the best of
their freshly baked items.

3. Antic Bocoi
📍 N4 🏠 Baixada de Viladecols 4
📞 93 310 50 57
Delicious Catalan *cocas* (a kind of
flat bread) are served with various
toppings in this lovely spot. There's
also a great value set lunch.

4. Elsa y Fred
📍 Q2 🏠 C/Rec Comtal 11
🌐 elsayfred.es
With its leather armchairs and big
windows, Elsa y Fred is the perfect
place to enjoy a long, lazy brunch,
with dishes ranging from classic
patates braves to salmon sushi.

5. Tetería Salterio
📍 M4 🏠 C/Sant Domenec del Call 4
📞 93 302 50 28 🕐 Mon–Fri D
Sample some excellent tea and sweet
Arab cakes at Tetería Salterio. Don't miss
the *sardo*, a flatbread-style dish with a
variety of toppings.

6. Bistrot Levante
📍 M3 🏠 Placeta de Manuel Ribé
📞 93 858 2679
Tuck into babka or avocado toast for
breakfast, or kofta and hummus at
lunch, at this chic hideaway. The terrace
is a perfect spot on a temperate day.

Popular Bar del Pla, known for its
delectable tapas

7. En Aparté
📍 P2 🏠 C/Lluís el Piadós 2
🌐 enaparte.es
With outside tables overlooking
the square, this relaxed café offers
French dishes and wines, good coffee
and brunch (Sat and Sun).

8. Caelum
📍 M3 🏠 C/Palla 8 📞 93 302 69 93
Up the stairs of this shop you will
find preserves and other foods,
all made in Spain's convents and
monasteries. Sample the delicacies downstairs at the site of the
15th-century baths.

9. La Granja Pallaresa
📍 L3 🏠 C/Petritxol 11
📞 93 302 20 36
This family-run *xocolateria* has
long been serving up thick, dark
hot chocolate. Don't forget to get
a side of *xurros* (fried, sugary dough
strips) to dunk in your mug of
hot chocolate.

10. Bar del Pla
📍 P4 🏠 C/Montcada 2 📞 93 268
30 03 🕐 Sun
Savour Spanish tapas with a French
twist at Bar del Pla. Try the pig's
trotters with *foie gras* or the squid
ink croquettes.

Restaurants and Tapas Bars

PRICE CATEGORIES

For a three-course meal for one with half a bottle of wine (or equivalent meal), taxes and extra charges

€ under €35 €€ €35–€50 €€€ over €50

1. Flax & Kale Passage

📍 P2 🏠 C/Sant Pere mes Alt 31–33
🌐 flaxandkale.com · €€

Part of a small chain of restaurants focusing on healthy, organic food (usually vegan or vegetarian), this venue is tucked down an atmospheric passage.

2. Cal Pep

📍 P5 🏠 Pl de les Olles 8 🕐 Sun, Mon L, last three weeks of Aug
🌐 calpep.com · €€

Taste a variety of delicious tapas, including the finest seafood, at this busy, established restaurant.

3. Cafè-Bar L'Antiquari

📍 N4 🏠 C/Veguer 13 📞 93 461 95 89 · €€€

Dig into beautifully plated food at this relaxed, rustic spot overlooking a medieval square.

4. Casa Delfín

📍 P4 🏠 Passeig del Born 36
🌐 casadelfinrestaurant.com · €€

This pretty bistro uses seasonal produce in imaginative dishes and tapas. The fried artichokes with *romesco* sauce are a must.

5. Llamber

📍 P4 🏠 C/Fusina 5 🌐 llamber.com · €€

Enjoy modern Spanish cuisine made with fresh seasonal produce, including homegrown vegetables and Mediterranean red prawns, in a loft-style interior. Also on offer is a wine menu with 30 wines by the glass and 150 by the bottle.

6. Fismuler

📍 Q2 🏠 C/Rec Comtal 17
🌐 fismuler.com · €€

This relaxed restaurant is known for some of the most inventive and exquisitely presented cuisine in the city. Don't miss the mozzarella salad with leek and hazelnut crumble.

7. Bodega La Palma

📍 M4 🏠 Palma de Sant Just 7
🕐 Sun 🌐 bodegalapalma.com · €

Set in a former wine cellar, Bodega La Palma offers a wide range of tapas, including stuffed Piquillo peppers.

8. Rasoterra

📍 M4 🏠 C/Palau 5 🕐 Sun D, Mon, Tue–Fri L 🌐 rasoterra.cat · €€

Proponents of the slow food movement, the owners of this stylish loft-style restaurant serve great vegetarian and vegan dishes along with organic wines and beer.

9. El Xampanyet

📍 P4 🏠 C/Montcada 22 📞 93 319 70 03 🕐 Sat D, Mon · €

An old-fashioned bar popular for its *cava* and simple but tasty tapas.

10. Govinda

📍 M2 🏠 Pl Vila de Madrid 4
🕐 Sun–Thu 🌐 govinda.es · €

A simple restaurant, Govinda serves vegetarian Indian dishes and delectable desserts, but no alcohol.

The elegant loft-style interior of Rasoterra

EL RAVAL

The sleek Museu d'Art Contemporani (MACBA) sits near ramshackle tenements; Asian groceries sell spices next to what were once Europe's most decadent brothels; art galleries share narrow streets with smoky old bars – this is a traditional working-class neighbourhood in flux. Since the 1990s it has been undergoing an enthusiastic urban renewal. Although the area has become a magnet for the city's young and hip crowd, it has managed to retain its unique character and still has plenty of edge.

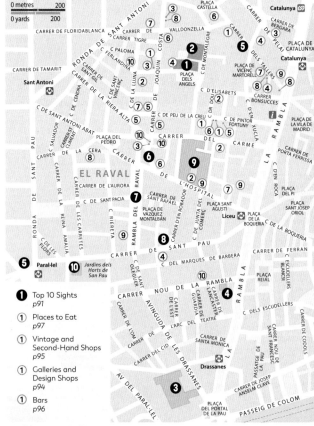

1 Top 10 Sights
p91

1 Places to Eat
p97

1 Vintage and Second-Hand Shops
p95

1 Galleries and Design Shops
p94

1 Bars
p96

For places to stay in this area, see p144

Striking façade of Barcelona's Museu d'Art Contemporani

1 Museu d'Art Contemporani (MACBA)

An eclectic array of work by big-name Spanish and international artists is gathered in this contemporary art hub (p42), housed inside a glass-fronted building designed by American architect Richard Meier. Excellent temporary exhibitions display everything from mixed media to sculpture and photography. Opposite stands the Gothic-style 16th-century Convent dels Àngels, built by Bartomeu Roig for the Dominican Tertiary Sisters. This is now used by Capella MACBA for temporary exhibitions, but long-term plans are to extend the galleries and exhibit some of MACBA's collection here permanently.

2 Centre de Cultura Contemporània (CCCB)

Housed in the 18th-century Casa de la Caritat, the CCCB is a focal point for the city's thriving contemporary art scene (p42). It hosts innovative art exhibitions, literature festivals, film screenings and lectures. A medieval courtyard is dazzlingly offset by a massive angled glass wall, artfully designed to reflect the city's skyline.

3 Museu Marítim
🚇 K6 🏛 Av de les Drassanes
🕙 10am–8pm daily (Nov–Mar: to 5:30pm) 🌐 mmb.cat 🚻 ♿

Barcelona's seafaring legacy comes to life at this museum, located in the beautifully restored Gothic shipyards. Admire the Gothic arches, where the

royal ships were once built, and the full-scale replica of the *Real*, a 16th-century fighting galley. You can also explore the *Santa Eulàlia (p106)*, a 1918 schooner moored at the Moll de la Fusta, and even board the boat for a sailing trip around the seafront (check website for timings and advance booking).

4 Palau Güell
🚇 L4 🏛 C/Nou de la Rambla 3–5
🕙 10am–8pm Tue–Sun (Nov–Mar: to 5:30pm; last adm: 1 hr before closing)
🌐 palauguell.cat ♿

In 1886, Count Güell asked Gaudí to build him a mansion that would set him apart from his neighbours. The result is the Palau Güell, one of Gaudí's earliest commissions. The interior is darker and less playful than his later works, but stained-glass panels and windows make the most of the light. The rooms are arranged around a huge central salon topped with a domed ceiling. The charming roof terrace hints at La Pedrera, another Gaudí work.

The richly decorated central salon at the Palau Güell

5 Avinguda Paral·lel
🗺 B3–D5

This avenue was home to the city's liveliest theatre and cabaret halls at the turn of the 20th century, and, despite being badly bombed in the Civil War, it remains the centre of the theatre district. A few of the pre-war theatres survive, including the landmark El Molino music hall, which dates from 1898, and the century-old Teatro Arnau – both are awaiting renovation, but there are plans afoot to convert them into cultural centres.

6 Carrers dels Tallers and de la Riera Baixa
🗺 L1 & K3

Looking for that retro look or a unique vintage piece of clothing? Along Carrers dels Tallers and de la Riera Baixa in the heart of El Raval are several vintage music and clothing shops selling everything from vinyl records and the latest CDs to original Hawaiian shirts. Best of all, many shops calculate the price by the weight of the clothes bought. On Saturdays, Carrer de la Riera Baixa has its own market (open 11am–8:30pm), when its stores display their wares on the street.

7 La Rambla del Raval
🗺 K4

This pedestrian walkway, lined with palm trees, started as an attempt by city planners to create an environment similar to that of the famed La Rambla (p26). As such, Rambla del Raval is lined with trendy bars and cafés, making it a rival to its more famous cousin for snacking and people-watching. Beyond this, the street also includes the striking, conical Barceló Hotel, with its panoramic rooftop terrace, and the sleek Filmoteca, a film archive complete with café and cinema. Halfway down the street, Botero's huge, plump bronze *Cat* usually has several neighbourhood kids crawling over its back.

8 Filmoteca
🗺 K4 🏠 Pl de Salvador Seguí 1–9 🌐 filmoteca.cat

The Filmoteca – the Catalan film archive – occupies a huge contemporary building just off the Rambla del Raval and has played a large part in the ongoing regeneration of this neighbourhood. It has two screening rooms and shows a varied programme. This includes film cycles dedicated to the finest directors from around the world, documentaries, Catalan films and special events for kids. It's extremely popular, not least because prices are very reasonable. There is also a café, a library specializing in film, a documentation centre and an in-demand terrace. On the first Sunday of the month, a flea market is held in the square outside.

The impressive entrance of the Antic Hospital de la Santa Creu

9 Antic Hospital de la Santa Creu

🗺 K3 ⬛ Entrances on C/Carme and at C/Hospital 56 ⬛ Courtyard: 9am–8pm daily

This Gothic hospital complex, now home to the National Library and various cultural organizations, dates from 1401 and is a reminder of the neighbourhood's medieval past (p94). Visitors should take a leisurely stroll through a pleasant garden surrounded by Gothic pillars, but a reader's card is needed for admission to the library. The elegant chapel has been converted into a wonderful contemporary art space.

10 Església de Sant Pau del Camp

🗺 J4 ⬛ C/Sant Pau 101 ⬛ 10am–5pm Mon–Sat

Deep in the heart of El Raval is this Romanesque church, one of the oldest in Barcelona. Originally founded as a Benedictine monastery in the 9th century and subsequently rebuilt, this ancient church is home to a lovely 12th-century cloister with intricately designed arches and beautiful capitals.

Tree-lined La Rambla del Raval, a beautiful pedestrianized street

A RAMBLE IN EL RAVAL

Carrer de Joaquin Costa
MACBA, CCCB
Plaça dels Àngels
Bar Muy Buenas
Rambla del Raval
Fernando Botero's Cat
Filmoteca
Marsella
Palau Güell
Església de Sant Pau del Camp

Morning

Choose an exhibition that appeals at either **MACBA** or the **CCCB** (p42), the city's two most important institutions of contemporary art and culture, which sit right next to each other. Watch the skateboarders on the **Plaça dels Àngels** or relax in the café overlooking the courtyard. Take C/Joaquin Costa down to the palm-lined **Rambla del Raval** for a stroll and admire Fernando Botero's Cat. The Rambla is packed with food spots: pick one for lunch, or go to the café in the **Filmoteca**, located just off the Rambla.

Afternoon

At the bottom of the Rambla, turn right on C/Sant Pau towards the Romanesque monastery of **Església de Sant Pau del Camp**. Admire the simple church and its miniature cloister with carved columns. Then walk back along C/Sant Pau, turning right when you reach the Rambla, then left on C/Nou de la Rambla. At No 3 stands Gaudí's **Palau Güell** (p91), an extravagant mansion that was one of his first commissions for the Güells. It has been beautifully restored, with its lavish salons and rooftop open to visitors. Kick off the evening with an absinthe at one of Barcelona's oldest bars, the **Marsella** (p96), before heading to the nearby **Bar Muy Buenas** (p96), which is decorated with Modernista details.

Galleries and Design Shops

1. Galeria dels Àngels
🚇 L2 🏠 C/Pintor Fortuny 27
🕐 11am–2pm Mon–Fri, 5–8pm
Sat 🌐 angelsbarcelona.com

Works of emerging and established
artists are showcased at this painting,
photography and sculpture gallery.

2. Miscelanea
🚇 L2 🏠 C/Dr Dou 16 🕐 11:30am–
8:30pm Mon–Sat 🌐 miscelanea.info

Miscelanea is an artists' project. It is
a multifunctional space, with a gallery
for exhibitions featuring works by
emerging artists, a shop selling design
objects and a café.

3. Siesta
🚇 K2 🏠 C/Ferlandina 18
🕐 11am–2pm & 5–8:30pm
Mon–Fri 🌐 siestaweb.com

Part boutique, part art gallery, Siesta
sells unique ceramics, jewellery and
glass art. It also hosts exhibitions.

4. MACBA Store Laie
🚇 K2 🏠 Plaça dels Àngels 1
🕐 10am–8pm Wed–Mon (to
3pm Sun) 🌐 macba.cat/en/
visit/store-library

This museum bookshop has a range
of designer gifts, including stationery,
homeware, toys and games as well as
books on art.

5. Grey Street
🚇 K2 🏠 C/Peu de la Creu 25
🕐 11am–3pm & 4–8pm Mon–Sat
🌐 greystreetbarcelona.com

A lovingly curated shop, Grey Street
sells mostly locally made gifts and
crafts, from stationery to jewellery
and bags.

6. HeyShop
🚇 L2 🏠 C/Dr Dou 4 🕐 11am–7pm
Mon–Sat (to 8pm Sat) 🌐 heyshop.es

Pick up prints, notebooks, T-shirts and
more at this design and illustra-
tion studio.

7. Imanol Ossa
🚇 K2 🏠 C/Peu de la Creu 24
🕐 Hours vary, chech website
🌐 imanolossa.com

Lamps, jewellery, and mobiles are
made from all kinds of upcycled
treasures at this studio run by a
young designer.

8. Fantastik
🚇 K1 🏠 C/Joaquin Costa 62
📞 93 301 30 68 🕐 11am–2pm &
4–8pm Mon–Sat

A colourful array of covetable items
from around the world, including
bright Mexican fabrics and rugs
from India, are available here at
affordable prices.

9. La Capella
🚇 K3 🏠 C/Hospital 56 🕐 Hours
vary, chech website 🌐 lacapella.
barcelona/ca

The Gothic chapel at the Antic
Hospital de la Santa Creu *(p93)*
now houses this contemporary art
gallery run by the city and dedicated
to emerging artists.

10. Ceràmica Marina Leal
🚇 K4 🏠 C/Nou de la Rambla 22
📞 93 412 71 80

Among the colourful jumble of
ceramics here, you'll find traditional Spanish jugs, plates, mugs
and much more.

**The austere exterior of the Gothic
La Capella art gallery**

Vintage and Second-Hand Shops

Browsing vintage clothing at vibrant Holala Tallers

Holala Tallers
📍L1 🏠C/Tallers 73 ☎93 302 05
03 ⏰11am–9pm Mon–Sat, noon–
5:30pm & 4:30–8pm Sun

Rummage for an outfit at this three-floor vintage store, with everything from silk kimonos to army pants and colourful 1950s bathing suits.

Flamingos
📍K2 🏠C/de Ferlandina 20
☎93 182 43 87 ⏰Noon–8pm
Mon–Sat

This fascinating vintage store, also selling old posters and bric-a-brac, operates on a weight system: you pay per kilo, depending on the clothing category.

Fusta'm
📍K1 🏠C/Joaquim Costa 62
☎639 527 076 ⏰11am–2pm &
5–8pm Mon–Fri

Discover second-hand furniture, lighting and decorative objects from around the world in the style of the 1950s, 60s and 70s at the eclectic Fusta'm. All the pieces sold have been completely restored at the store's workshop.

4. Revólver Records
📍L2 🏠C/Tallers 11 ☎93 412 73 58
⏰10am–9pm Mon–Sat

The speciality here is classic rock, and the wall art fittingly depicts The Rolling Stones and Jimi Hendrix. One floor houses CDs, the other vinyl.

5. Wilde Sunglasses Store
📍K2 🏠C/Joaquin Costa 2
⏰1–8:30pm Mon–Sat

This dimly-lit boutique is lined with all kinds of vintage-style sunglasses.

6. Holala Plaça
📍E3 🏠Pl Castella 2 ☎93 302 05 93
⏰11am–9pm Mon–Sat

Shop for second-hand clothes, furniture and bric-a-brac at this huge store.

7. La Principal Retro & Co
📍K2 🏠C/Ferlandina 37 ☎60 726 57
57 ⏰Noon–3pm & 4–8pm Mon–Sat

Set in a charming old dairy, this chic boutique offers a huge range of fantastic vintage T-shirts.

8. Soul BCN
📍L1 🏠C/Tallers 15 ☎93 481 32 94
⏰11am–8:30pm Mon–Sat

A vintage-style shop, Soul BCN sells 1950s frocks, sunglasses, Bardot tops and much more.

9. Discos Tesla
📍L2 🏠C/Tallers 3 ☎664 095 091
⏰9:30am–9pm Mon–Sat

This record and CD store focuses on alternative music from decades past. Visitors can hum a few lines of a song and the owner will track it down.

10. Lullaby
📍K3 🏠C/Riera Baixa 22
☎93 443 08 02

You will find all sorts of treasures in this quirky little boutique, from floaty frocks to vintage sportswear, along with some fabulous jewellery and handbags.

Bars

1. Bar Almirall
📍 J4 🏠 C/Joaquín Costa 33
🕐 Hours vary, check website
🌐 casaalmirall.com

The city's oldest bar, Almirall was founded in 1860. Today, it retains many of its original fittings and is popular for its eclectic music and strong cocktails.

2. El Jardí
📍 K3 🏠 C/Hospital 56 📞 93 681 92 34 🕐 1–11pm daily

Escape the crowds in this peaceful outdoor café-bar, overlooking a garden. Go for the *vermut* (vermouth) and some olives.

3. La Confitería
📍 J4 🏠 C/Sant Pau 2 🕐 Hours vary, check website 🌐 confiteria.cat

Set in a former sweet shop, this bar has original Modernista fittings. Tasty cocktails and tapas are on the menu.

4. Marsella
📍 K4 🏠 C/Sant Pau 65 📞 34 934 42 72 63 🕐 daily (to 1:30am Fri–Sat)

A dimly lit Modernista bar, Marsella serves cocktails and absinthe to regulars and first-timers.

5. Two Shmucks
📍 K2 🏠 C/Joaquín Costa 52
📞 674 480 073

This buzzy neighbourhood bar made it onto the 50 Best Bars in the world. Venture in and you'll see why – every night has a different theme, and the imaginative cocktail menu changes regularly.

6. Betty Ford's
📍 K1 🏠 C/Joaquin Costa 56 🕐 5pm–2am daily 🌐 bettyfordsbcn.com

Named after the Hollywood set's favourite rehab and detox centre, this cocktail bar has a 1950s vibe.

Modernista decor at the iconic Bar Muy Buenas

7. Bar Kasparo
📍 L2 🏠 Pl Vicenç Martorell 4
📞 34 933 02 20 72 🕐 9am–midnight daily

During the day, this charming bar is a favourite with local families, but come dusk it's a fabulous place to chill out over a glass of wine.

8. Boadas Cocktail Bar
📍 L2 🏠 C/Tallers 1 🕐 Noon–1:30am Tue–Sat 🌐 boadascocktails.com

Founded in 1933, the charming Boadas Cocktail Bar continues to mix the best martinis in town.

9. Bar Palosanto
📍 K4 🏠 Rambla de Raval 26
🕐 6–11:30pm Mon, Thu–Sun

A colourful café-bar with a few outdoor tables, this is a cosy spot for drinks, tapas and light meals.

10. Bar Muy Buenas
📍 K2 🏠 C/del Carme 63 🕐 Noon–midnight daily 🌐 muybuenas.cat

An iconic Modernista-era bar, Muy Buenas was established in 1928 and is set in a building that dates back to 189● It serves cocktails, spirits and over 30 wines made in Catalonia. Don't forget to sample some of the refined tapas and Catalan classics on the menu.

Places to Eat

1. Caravelle
L2 **C/Pintor Fortuny 31** D
caravellebcn.com · €

This spot near the MACBA *(p42)* has become a favourite for weekend brunch and long coffee breaks. The menu changes regularly but is likely to include delicious *huevos rancheros* and vegetarian options.

2. Superclàssic
L3 **C/Floristes de la Rambla 14**
93 197 78 29 · €

On offer at this spot are a mix of classic and more inventive tapas, including veggie and vegan options. Grab a seat on the terrace overlooking the square.

3. La Esquina
L1 **C/Bergara 2** **laesquina barcelona.com** · €

The spacious La Esquina serves all-day brunch and light lunch fare such as pulled pork tacos and Caesar salad.

4. Bacaro
L3 **C/Jerusalém 6** Sun
bacarobarcelona.com · €€

Tucked behind the Boqueria market, this convivial little Italian restaurant-bar serves modern Venetian cuisine.

5. Biocenter
L2 **C/Pintor Fortuny 25**
Hours vary, chech website
restaurantebiocenter.es · €

At this vegetarian restaurant, dishes are prepared with organic produce. There's an array of dishes to choose from, including amazing desserts (vegan, gluten-free and sugar-free options are available).

6. A Tu Bola
K3 **C/de Hospital 78**
93 315 32 44 Tue · €€

A local favourite, A Tu Bola is well known for its fish, meat and vege-table balls served between bread with a range of dips and sauces.

PRICE CATEGORIES
For a three-course meal for one with half a bottle of wine (or equivalent meal), taxes and extra charges

€ under €35 €€ €35–€50 €€€ over €50

7. Teresa Carles
L1 **C/Jovellanos 2** **teresa carles.com** · €

The flagship of a small chain of healthy food restaurants, Teresa Carles offers imaginative vegetarian fare, such as crêpes with artichokes and brie.

8. Cera 23
J3 **C/Cera 23** **7:30–11pm Fri–Tue** **cera23.com** · €€

A stylish Galician restaurant, Cera 23 serves northern Spain's classic dishes with a contemporary twist.

9. El Quim de la Boqueria
L3 **Local 606, La Rambla 93**
Hours vary, chech website
elquimdelaboqueria.com · €

One of Boqueria's best counter bars, this serves Catalan classics with a twist.

10. L'Havana
K2 **C/Lleó 1** Sun D, Mon, 4 wks in Jul & Aug **restauranthavana.cat** · €€

This restaurant specializes in superb Catalan cuisine. Try the fresh fish of the day or dishes such as pig's trotters. The set lunch menu is excellent too.

A platter of plant-based food at Teresa Carles

MONTJUÏC

Named the "Jewish Mountain" after an important Jewish cemetery that existed here in the Middle Ages, this sizable park was first landscaped for the International Exhibition in 1929, when the Palau Nacional and the Mies van der Rohe Pavilion were also constructed. Buildings were erected all over the north side, with the grand Avinguda de la Reina María Cristina leading onto the base of the hill from the Plaça d'Espanya. However, the area soon fell into general disuse, becoming synonymous with decline. With the grim shadow left by Castell de Montjuïc, which for years acted as a slaughterhouse for Franco's firing squads, it is little short of miraculous that Montjuïc is now one of the city's biggest draws.

As the site for the 1992 Olympics, it was transformed into a beautiful green oasis, with fabulous museums and sports facilities all connected by a network of outdoor escalators and interlaced with quiet, shady gardens.

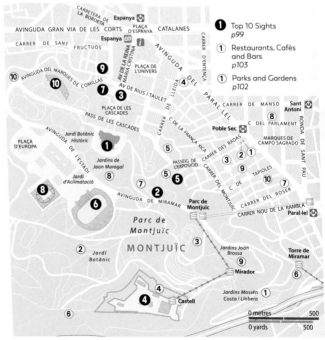

1 Top 10 Sights p99

1 Restaurants, Cafés and Bars p103

1 Parks and Gardens p102

For places to stay in this area, see p145

Palau Nacional and the Font Màgica lit up at night

Palau Nacional and Museu Nacional d'Art e Catalunya

e Palau Nacional is home to the useu Nacional d'Art de Catalunya 30), which exhibits Catalonia's storic art collections. Home to e of Europe's finest displays of omanesque art, the museum cludes a series of 12th-century escoes, rescued from Catalan renean churches and painstak-gly reassembled in a remarkable ries of galleries.

Fundació Joan Miró

One of Catalonia's most claimed painters and sculptors, an Miró (1893–1983) donated any of the 14,000 works held by is museum (*p36*). Housed in a stark ite building designed by his end, architect Josep Lluís Sert, is the world's most complete llection of the artist's work.

Font Màgica

B4 Pl Carles Buigas 1 (off Reina Maria Cristina) Shows: r, May & first 2 whs of Oct barcelona.cat/ca/que-pots-r-a-bcn/font-magica

low the many cascades and fountains at descend from the Palau Nacional he Magic Fountain, designed by

Carles Buigas for the International Exhibition of 1929. As darkness falls, countless jets of water are choreo-graphed in a mesmerizing sound and light show. When the water meets in a single jet it can soar to 15 m (50 ft). The finale is often accompanied by a recording of Freddie Mercury and soprano Montserrat Caballé singing the anthem *Barcelona* as the water fades from pink to green and back to white. The Four Columns behind the fountain represent the Catalan flag and are a symbol of the Catalanism movement. Note that water restrictions in times of drought may affect timings and performances at Font Màgica.

4 Castell de Montjuïc

B6 Carretera de Montjuïc 66 10am–6pm daily (Apr–Oct: to 8pm) ajuntament.barcelona.cat/castelldemontjuic

Dominating Montjuïc's hill, this castle was once a prison and torture centre for political prisoners. Its darkest moment came at the end of the Spanish Civil War when 4,000 Catalan nationalists and republicans were shot in the nearby Fossar de la Pedrera. The museum explores the history of Montjuïc, as well as the role of the castle in the Civil War. Visitors can still climb the fort's bastions for superb views of the port below.

5 Teatre Grec

🔲 C4 🏛 Pg Santa Madrona
🕙 10am–dusk daily 🌐 barcelona.cat/grec ♿

At the foot of Montjuic is this remarkable outdoor amphitheatre that was once a quarry. The design of the theatre was inspired by the Classical ideas of Noucentisme, a late 19th-century Catalan architectural movement that was a reaction to the decorative nature of Modernisme. The leafy green backdrop and beautiful gardens make for an enchanting place for an afternoon's stroll or meal at the luxurious restaurant. During the summertime, the theatre hosts jazz acts and shows such as Swan Lake as part of the Grec Festival (p75).

6 Estadi Olímpic

🔲 B5 🏛 Av de l'Estadi 60
🕙 Museum: 10am–6pm Tue–Sun (to 2:30pm Sun, Apr–Sep: to 7:30pm) 🌐 estadiolimpic.barcelona ♿

The stadium was first built for the 1936 Workers' Olympics, which were cancelled with the outbreak of the Spanish Civil War (p11). The original Neo-Classical façade is still in place, but the stadium was rebuilt for the 1992 Olympic Games (p11). The interactive Museu Olímpic i de l'Esport nearby is dedicated to all aspects of sport. You can also view the stadium from the upper levels.

7 Pavelló Mies van der Rohe

🔲 B4 🏛 Av Francesc Ferrer i Guàrdia 7 🕙 10am–8pm daily (Nov–Feb: to 6pm) 🌐 miesbcn.com ♿

You might wonder exactly what this box-like pavilion of stone, marble, onyx and glass is doing in the middle of Montjuïc's monumental architecture. This architectural gem was Germany's contribution to the 1929 International Exhibition. Built by Ludwig Mies van der Rohe (1886–1969), the Rationalist pavilion was soon demolished, only to be reconstructed in 1986. Inside, the sculpture *Morning* by Georg Kolbe (1877–1947) is reflected in a small lake.

8 Palau Sant Jordi

🔲 A4 🏛 Pg Olímpic 5–7
🕙 For events only, chech website 🌐 palausantjordi.barcelona

The biggest star of all the Olympic facilities is this steel-and-glass indoor stadium (closed to the public) and multipurpose installation designed by Japanese architect Arata Isozaki. Holding around 17,000 people, the stadium is the home of the city's basketball team. The esplanade – a surreal forest of concrete and metal pillars – was designed by Aiko Isozaki, Arata's wife. Further down the hill are the indoor and outdoor Bernat Picornell Olympic pools, both of which are open to the public.

9 CaixaForum

🔲 B3 🏛 Av Francesc Ferrer i Guàrdia 6–8 🕙 10am–8pm daily 🌐 caixaforum.es ♿

The Fundació La Caixa's impressive collection of contemporary art is housed in a former textile factory

Teatre Grec, a remarkable outdoor amphitheatre

built in 1911 by Catalan Modernista architect Puig i Cadafalch. Restored and opened as a gallery in 2002, it assembles almost 800 works by Spanish and foreign artists, shown in rotation along with temporary international exhibitions. The roof terrace offers exceptional views of the city.

10 Poble Espanyol

📍 A3 📍 Av Francesc Ferrer i Guàrdia 🕐 10am–8pm Mon, 10am–midnight Tue–Thu & Sun, 9am–3am Fri, 9am–4pm Sat 🌐 poble-espanyol.com 📍

This Spanish *poble* (village) features famous buildings and streets from around Spain recreated in full-scale. It has become a centre for arts and crafts, with an impressive glass-blowers' workshop and many shops selling local crafts. The addition of several pretty restaurants and cafés have made the village one of the city's more popular attractions.

A picture-perfect arched alley in Poble Espanyol

A DAY IN MONTJUÏC

Morning

To get to the **Fundació Joan Miró** (p36) before the crowds and with energy to spare, hop on an early funicular from Paral·lel metro station. It's a short walk from the funicular to the museum, where you'll need an hour and a half to absorb the collection of Miró paintings, sketches and sculptures. When you've had your fill of art, refuel with a *cafè amb llet* (milky coffee) at the restaurant before back-tracking along Av de Miramar and jumping on the cable car up to **Castell de Montjuïc** (p99). Wander the castle gardens and look out over the city and the docks. Return to Av de Miramar by cable car and either pop back in to the Miró Foundation for a lunch at the café (note there aren't many eating options in Montjuïc) or enjoy the set lunch at the restaurant in the **Palau Nacional** (p99).

Afternoon

After lunch, spend time admiring the extraordinary Romanesque art collection at **MNAC** (p30). When you exit, turn right and follow the signs to the Olympic complex. Wander past the **Estadi Olímpic** and the silver-domed **Palau Sant Jordi**, which steals the limelight. Spend the late afternoon cooling down with a dip in the fantastic open-air pool at nearby Bernat Picornell. From here it is a short stroll to the **Poble Espanyol**, where you can settle in at a terrace bar in Plaça Major.

Parks and Gardens

1. Jardins Mossèn Costa i Llobera
🅟 C5 🚊 C/de Miramar 38 🕐 10am–dush daily

These are among Europe's most important cactus and succulent gardens. They are particularly impressive as the sun sets, when surreal shapes and shadows emerge.

2. Jardí Botànic
🅟 A5 🚊 C/Dr Font i Quer 2 🕐 10am–8pm daily (Oct–Mar: to 5pm) 🌐 museuciencies.cat ♿

Barcelona's botanical gardens are found among the stadiums used in the 1992 Olympics. Dating from 1999, the gardens contain hundreds of examples of typical Mediterranean flora. Don't miss the Jardí Botànic Històric nearby.

3. Jardins Mossèn Cinto Verdaguer
🅟 C5 🚊 Av Miramar 30 🕐 10am–dush daily

The best time to visit these elegant gardens is during spring, when the plants are in blossom and the colours and scents are in full force.

4. Jardins del Castell
🅟 B5 🚊 C/de Montjuïc 66

Cannons dotted among the rose bushes along the walls of a flower-filled moat are the highlights of these gardens which ring the castle.

5. Jardins del Teatre Grec
🅟 C4 🚊 Pg Santa Madrona 38

Reminiscent of the Hanging Gardens of Babylon, this oasis surrounding the Greek amphitheatre is officially known as La Rosadela.

6. Jardins de Miramar
🅟 D5 🚊 C/Dr Font i Quer 2

Opposite the Miramar hotel, these gardens are scattered with stairways leading to leafy groves with vistas across the city and the port area.

Jardins de Joan Brossa, named after the famous Catalan poet

7. Jardins Laribal
🅟 B4 🚊 Pg Santa Madrona 2 🕐 10am–dush daily

This multilevel park hides a small Modernista house by architect Puig i Cadafalch and the Font del Gat, a drinking fountain that has inspired many local songs.

8. Jardins de Joan Maragall
🅟 B4 🚊 Av Estadi 69 🕐 10am–3pm Sat & Sun

An avenue lined with sculptures by Frederic Marès and Ernest Maragall is the main delight in the Jardins de Joan Maragall, which also has the last of the city's *ginjoler* trees.

9. Jardins de Joan Brossa
🅟 C5 🚊 Pl de Dante 9999 🕐 10am–dush daily

The variety of grasses and trees alone make Joan Brossa gardens truly fascinating. A cross between city gardens and a woodland park, these gardens come into their own in spring, but are popular all year – thanks to the musical instruments, climbing frames and a flying fox.

10. El Mirador del Llobregat
🅟 A3

A viewing area with small gardens nearby, this is the only place in the city where you can see the plains of the Llobregat stretching below.

Restaurants, Cafés and Bars

PRICE CATEGORIES
For a three-course meal for one with half a bottle of wine (or equivalent meal), taxes and extra charges

€ under €35 €€ €35–€50 €€€ over €50

1. Malabida
C4 · C/Blai 63 · 93 175 81 79
Sun & Mon · €
A welcoming spot, Malabida offers simple tapas, hearty sandwiches and platters of cheese and charcuterie.

2. Mano Roto
C4 · C/Creu dels Molers 4 · Mon–Fri D · manorota.net · €€€
The seasonal dishes at this stylish bistro are a creative fusion of Catalan, Japanese and Peruvian cuisines.

3. El Sortidor
C4 · Pl del Sortidor 5 · 690 765 721 · Mon · €
Featuring original stained-glass doors and tiled floors from 1908, El Sortidor serves tasty meals in a romantic setting.

4. Alapar
C4 · C/Lleida 5 · Tue, Wed, Sun D · alaparbcn.com · €€
Innovative Japanese-Mediterranean fusion dishes are the draw here.

5. El Lliure
B4 · Pg Santa Madrona 40–46 · 664 862 623 · Mon–Fri D, Sat L (except on days with performances) · €
The Lliure theatre has a café with an adjoining restaurant and terrace area, ideal for having a meal before a show.

6. La Caseta del Migdia
B6 · Mirador del Migdia · Apr–Sep: Mon & Tue; Oct–Mar: Mon–Fri · €
Leave the city behind and head for this lofty outdoor bar at the top of Montjuïc, where you can enjoy ice-cold drinks, a welcome breeze and amazing views: the bar has one of the best sunset views in the city.

7. La Federica
D4 · C/de Salvà 3 · 93 600 59 01 · Mon & Tue · €
A vintage-style bar, La Federica serves brunch as well as an array of imaginative tapas to go with a wide range of cocktails.

8. Bar Calders
C4 · C/Parlament 25 · 93 329 93 49 · Mon–Thu L · €
This sought-after terrace spot is perfect for relaxing over a *vermut* (vermouth) or an expertly mixed gin and tonic.

9. O Meu Lar
C4 · C/Margarit 24 · 93 329 70 74 · Sun · €€
The walls of this traditional Galician restaurant are lined with old photos. The specialities here are tapas and charcoal-grilled meats.

10. Quimet & Quimet
C4 · C/Poeta Cabanyes 25 · 93 442 31 42 · Sat, Sun & three weeks in Aug · €
This tiny bodega has standing room only, but serves delicious tapas and wonderful wines.

The cosy tapas bar Quimet & Quimet, founded in 1914

THE SEAFRONT

The azure waters of the Mediterranean are only ever a few metro stops away. The city's beaches were once hidden behind an industrial wasteland, but things changed radically in preparation for the 1992 Olympics. As a result of the ambitious project to transform the city, the old industrial waterfront was demolished and a 4-km- (2-mile-) long stretch of promenades and sandy beaches was laid out. A marina was also constructed to host restaurants and bars. The plan was to create a city *oberta al mar* (open to the sea); the result is phenomenal. Scenic beaches and shady palm trees now stretch from Barceloneta, Barcelona's fishing village, to the yacht-filled Port Olímpic and beyond. Behind it is Poblenou, a once humble neighbourhood that has been transformed and is now a hub for tech companies and design studios. Just inland, the leafy expanse of the Parc de la Ciutadella, with its fountain and boating lake, is the perfect green retreat.

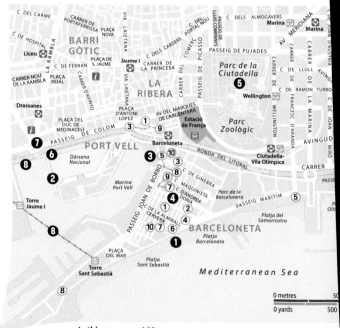

For places to stay in this area, see p146

Barceloneta beach filled with activity

1 Beaches
E6

For a splash in the Mediterranean, head down to the end of La Rambla, wander along the palm tree-lined Moll de la Fusta, and down the restaurant-packed Passeig Joan de Borbó, where the sea beckons. More than 7 km (4.3 miles) of blue-flag beaches stretch north from Barceloneta to Port Olímpic and beyond. The seawater quality can vary, depending on the tides. Facilities are top-notch, including showers, deckchairs, lifeguards and beach volleyball courts. The beachfront boardwalk is the perfect spot for a stroll. Look out for Rebecca Horn's sculpture, *L'Estel Ferit* (The Wounded Star), a local landmark.

2 Rambla de Mar
E5

Saunter along the Rambla de Mar, a floating wooden pier that leads to the flashy Maremagnum mall. It is open every day of the year, which makes it particularly popular with shoppers on Sundays.

3 Museu d'Història de Catalunya
N6 ☑ Pl Pau Vila 3 ⏰10am–7pm Tue–Sat (to 8pm Wed), 10am–2:30pm Sun ☑ mhcat.cat ☑

Housed in the Palau de Mar, a renovated portside warehouse, this museum offers a broad, interactive exploration of Catalonia's history since prehistoric times. Kids especially will have a ball with the engaging exhibits, such as a Civil War-era bunker and a recreated Catalan bar from the 1960s with an ancient *futbolín* (table football) game.

4 Barceloneta
F6

A portside warren of narrow streets, small squares and ancient bars, this neighbourhood of *pescadors* (fishers) and *mariners* (sailors) seems worlds apart from the mega-malls of nearby Port Olímpic. A foray through this tight-knit community yields a glimpse into the Barcelona of 150 years ago. Small seafood restaurants serve a *menú del migdia* of whatever is fresh off the boat. Running the length of Barceloneta's western edge is the Passeig Joan de Borbó, which is lined with restaurants serving *mariscs* (shellfish) and paellas.

- ❶ Top 10 Sights
  p105
- ① Restaurants and Cafés
  p109
- ① Bars and Tapas Bars
  p108

The *Quadriga de l'Aurora* on the fountain in Parc de la Ciutadella

5 Parc de la Ciutadella
🅿 R4 🏠 Pg Pujades
🕐 10am–10:30pm daily ♿

Colourful parrots take flight from the top of palm trees and bright orange groves are dotted around this famous park. A perfect picnic spot, the city's largest central green space is particularly popular on Sunday afternoons, when people gather to play instruments, relax, head out onto the boating lake for a punt, or visit the museum and the zoo. The northeastern corner of the park features a magnificent fountain – a cascading waterfall topped by a chariot rider flanked by griffins caught mid-roar.

6 Pailebot Santa Eulàlia
🅿 L6 🏠 Moll de la Fusta
🕐 Hours vary, chech website
🌐 mmb.cat ♿

Bobbing in the water at the Moll de la Fusta (Timber Quay) is this restored three-mast schooner, originally christened *Carmen Flores*. It first set sail from Spain in 1918. On journeys to Cuba, the ship used to transport textiles and salt, returning with tobacco, coffee, cereals and wood. In 1997, the Museu Marítim *(p91)* bought and restored the ship as part of a project to create a collection of seaworthy historical Catalan vessels.

7 Monument a Colom
🅿 E5 🏠 Pl Portal de la Pau
Ciutat Vella

This 60-m- (197-ft-) high col was built between 1882 an 1888 for Barcelona's Univ Exhibition and commem Christopher Columbus's voyage to the Americas; i in Barcelona that Columbus m Ferdinand and Isabel on his re Columbus's statue stands atop column, pointing out to sea, sup sedly towards the New World bu actually towards Italy. There hav calls to have the statue removed; Mayor Ada Colau pushed back, s the city should own up to its pas keep the statue as a reminder.

8 Boat and Cable-Car T
🅿 E5/6 🏠 Telefèric: from To San Sebastià; Las Golondrinas Portal de la Pau; Orsom: Porta la Pau 🕐 Every 30 mins from 11

Observe all the activity at Barce port area from a different persp either from the air or the sea. Th *Transbordador Aeri* cable cars ru Miramar station and San Sebast Tower, offering sweeping views o Barcelona and its coast. On the v the Las Golondrinas "swallow bo *(lasgolondrinas.com)* and the Ors Catamaran *(barcelona-orsom.com* regular sightseeing trips around harbour, the beaches and the po

A red Transbordador Aeri cable car soaring above Barcelona

9 Poblenou and Palo Alto Design Complex

H5 poblenouurbandistrict.com/en; paloalto.barcelona

The fashionable Poblenou district has become a hub for startups and tech companies. A burgeoning number of trendy cafés and shops have opened, contemporary buildings are sprouting up and the old industrial warehouses are being restored and repurposed. One contains BD Design, the city's most prestigious design showroom, while the Palo Alto complex houses the studios of several big-name designers.

10 Museu de Ciències Naturals

Pl Leonardo da Vinci 4–5, Parc del Fòrum Hours vary, chech website museuciencies.cat

The main site of the Museu de Ciències Naturals occupies a raised triangular building constructed by Herzog & de Meuron for Barcelona's Forum 2004 event. This is a family-friendly place, with an appealing mix of contemporary exhibits and old-fashioned cabinets full of stuffed animals. The main exhibition is a "biography of the earth", with interactive audiovisual displays about "the origins of the world". There is a special area for kids under seven to learn about science, plus a library and café. The Jardí Botànic (p102) is also part of the Museu de Ciències Naturals.

EXPLORING THE PORT

Morning

Begin your port passeig (stroll) with a visit to the **Museu Marítim** (p91), where you can sense Barcelona's status as one of the most active ports in the Mediterranean. From here, head towards the Monument a Colom and stroll along the Moll de la Fusta to admire the **Pailebot Santa Eulàlia**, which has been meticulously restored by the museum. Take a stroll down the **Rambla de Mar** (p105), an undulating wooden drawbridge that leads to the **Maremagnum** (p69) shopping mall. At the start of the pier, take a boat ride on the Orsom Catamaran, where you can grab a drink and a snack. Soak up the sunshine and the port skyline while sprawled out on a net just inches above the water. Back on land, stroll down the Moll d'Espanya and turn towards the traditional fisher's quarter of **Barceloneta**, an atmospheric pocket of narrow streets and timeworn bars. Get a real taste of old-style Barcelona at the lively tapas place, **El Vaso de Oro** (C/Balboa 6). Enjoy a drink at the bar and savour tasty seafood.

Afternoon

Head to Passeig Joan de Borbó and the beach. Douse yourself in the Med, then siesta in the afternoon sun. Pick yourself up with a drink at **Salamanca xiringuito** (at the end of Pg Joan de Borbó) or at one of the many beachside bars nearby.

The beautiful and sandy Mar bella beach

Bars and Tapas Bars

1. Mar Bella beach bars
📍 Platja Nova Mar Bella
🕐 Winter

Head to one of the *xiringuitos* (beach bars) found on Barcelona's hippest beach and enjoy the DJ sessions.

2. La Guingeta de l'Escribà
📍H6 📍 Av Litoral 62, Platja de Bogatell 🌐 restaurantse scriba.com

A beach bar right on the sand, this spot offers breakfast, tapas, light meals, cocktails and more.

3. Bar Jai Ca
📍 F5 📍 C/Ginebra 13 🌐 barjaica.com

This is a relaxed neighbourhood favourite. Delicious tapas and good wine are on offer.

4. Bodega Fermín
📍 F6 📍 C/Sant Carles 18 🕐 Noon–midnight daily (to 1am Fri & Sat)

Laid-back hangout, with craft beers on tap and a selection of simple, tasty tapas. It's a great place to enjoy a *vermut*, the preferred aperitif.

5. Noxe
📍 F6 📍 W Hotel, Pl de la Rosa dels Vents 1 🌐 noxebar celona.com

The spectacular bar on the 26th floor of the W Hotel (commonly known as the Hotel Vela) offers lovely views of the city. Note that the bar has a smart dress code.

6. Bus Terraza
📍 Parc del Fòrum, Av del Litoral 488
🕐 Hours vary, chech website 🌐 bus-terraza.com

There are regular DJ sessions and live jazz concerts at this converted double-decker bus.

7. L'Òstia
📍 F6 📍 Plaça de la Barceloneta 🌐 lostiabcn.com

A modern take on a classic tavern, this spot serves a fine array of traditional tapas as well as fresh seafood, which you can enjoy on the charming terrace.

8. La Bombeta
📍 F6 📍 C/Maquinista 33
📞 93 319 94 45

This popular Catalan bar offers a wonderful glimpse of life in Barcelona before the tourists arrived. The house speciality is the *bombas*, deep-fried balls of mashed potatoes served with a spicy meat-and-tomato sauce. Be prepared to wait for a table.

9. Bodega La Peninsula
📍 F5 📍 C/del Mar 29 📞 93 221 40 89

The old-fashioned Bodega La Peninsula serves fresh seafood and tapas made with local produce.

10. El Vaso de Oro
📍 F5 📍 C/Balboa 6 📞 93 319 30 98

A traditional bar, El Vaso de Oro has served ice-cold beer and fresh tapas for more than half a century. Grab a stool at the long, narrow counter early; it gets packed very quickly.

Restaurants and Cafés

1. Set Portes
N5 Pg Isabel II 14 7portes.com/en · €€
Founded in 1836, this legendary city institution has some of the finest Catalan cuisine in the city, including a variety of paellas.

2. El Filferro
F6 C/Sant Carles 29 600 83 66 74 Hours vary, call ahead · €
This charming café, with tables set on the square, is perfect for coffee and cake, a delicious light lunch of Mediterranean specialities or a *vermut* on a summer evening.

3. Green Spot
N5 C/Reina Cristina 12 grupotragaluz.com/the-green-spot · €€
A spacious restaurant with sleek, minimalist design, Green Spot serves some of the best vegan and vegetarian food in the city.

4. Barraca
G6 Pg. Marítim de la Barceloneta 1 barracabarcelona.com · €€
Enjoy lovely sea views from the huge windows of the dining room at this restaurant reputed for serving some of the best paellas in the city.

5. Brunch & Cake By The Sea
F5 Pg Joan de Borbó 5 93 138 35 72 Hours vary, call ahead · €
Furnished with a rustic decor, this bright café features an extensive brunch menu of classics such as eggs Benedict. Find delectable vegan and gluten-free options as well as homemade cakes.

6. Salamanca
F6 C/Almirall Cervera 34 restaurantesalamanca.es · €€
This may feel like a tourist trap at first, but the food is top-notch. There are plenty of meat dishes on offer.

7. La Roseta
F6 C/Meer 37 673 81 69 76 8:30am–2:30pm daily · €
A cosy spot that offers homemade cakes, including a legendary cheesecake, as well as great coffee.

8. El Gallito
F5 Passeig del Mare Nostrum 19 grupotragaluz.com/gallito · €€
This stylish spot offers a range of delicacies, including Mediterranean rice seafood dishes.

9. Oaxaca
F5 Pla de Palau 20 93 319 00 64 1–4pm & 7–11pm daily · €€
One of the best Mexican restaurants in the city, Oaxaca serves creative dishes such as *sopa azteca con tortillas* (soup) or quesadillas with spider crab.

10. La Mar Salada
E6 Pg de Joan de Borbó 58 93 221 21 27 Hours vary, call ahead · €€
Light and bright, this restaurant specializes in modern fare with an emphasis on seafood, such as monkfish with wild mushrooms and paella.

Exquisitely presented tàrtar de sorell at La Mar Salada

EIXAMPLE

If the old town is the heart of Barcelona, and green Tibidabo and Montjuïc its lungs, the Eixample is its nervous system, its economic and commercial core. The area took shape in 1860, when the city was finally allowed to expand beyond the medieval walls. Based on plans by Catalan engineer Ildefons Cerdà, the Eixample is laid out on a rigid grid system of streets. At each intersection the chamfered corners were cut off at a 45-degree angle, to allow the buildings there to overlook the junctions or squares. Construction continued into the 20th century at a time when the elite was patronizing the most daring architects. Modernisme was flourishing and the area became home to the best of Barcelona's Modernista architecture, with its elegant façades and balconies. Today, enchanting cafés, funky design shops, gourmet restaurants and hip bars draw the professional crowd, which has adopted the neighbourhood as its own.

1 Top 10 Sights p111

1 Restaurants and Tapas Bars p117

1 Design Shops p114

1 Bars p115

1 Cafés p116

For places to stay in this area, see p146

The Art Nouveau Sant Pau
Recinte Modernista complex

1 Sagrada Família
Gaudí's wizardry culminated in this enchanting and unconventional church (p22), which dominates the city skyline.

2 La Pedrera
A daring, surreal fantasyland, this apartment block is Gaudí's most remarkable civic work (p34).

3 Sant Pau Recinte Modernista
H1 **C/Sant Antoni Maria Claret 167** **Hours vary, chech website** **santpaubarcelona.org**

Founded in 1401, the Hospital de la Santa Creu i de Sant Pau was a fully-functioning hospital until 2009, when all medical activities were moved to a new building and the UNESCO World Heritage Site was restored and opened to the public as a cultural centre. The Art Nouveau site, created by Domènech i Montaner between 1902 and 1930, is a tribute to Modernisme – and his answer to Gaudí's Sagrada Família. There are eight pavilions, which house murals and sculptures, and other buildings, all linked by underground tunnels. The buildings are interlaced by gardens and courtyards. The site is part of the Ruta del Modernisme.

4 Mansana de la Discòrdia
E2 **Pg de Gràcia 35–45**

At the heart of the city's *Quadrat d'Or* (Golden Square) lies this stunning row of houses. The "Block of Discord" is so named because of the dramatic contrast between its three flagship buildings. Built between 1900 and 1907 by the three Modernista greats, rival architects Gaudí, Domènech i Montaner and Puig i Cadafalch, the houses were commissioned by competing bourgeois families. Domènech designed the ornate Casa Lleó Morera, Puig created the Gothic-inspired Casa Amatller (p50), and Gaudí built the whimsical Casa Batlló (p50). Among them, the Casa Amatller and Casa Batlló can be toured. The houses at Nos. 37 and 39 add to the splendour of the block. At No. 39 is the Museu del Perfum (p49).

Tàpies's striking *Cloud and Chair* sculpture on the Fundació Tàpies

5 Fundació Tàpies
📍 E2 📍 C/Aragó 255 🕐 10am–7pm Tue–Sat, 10am–3pm Sun 🌐 fundaciotapies.org 📱

Paintings and sculptures by Antoni Tàpies (1923–2012), Catalonia's foremost artist, are housed in this early Modernista building. For a glimpse of what awaits inside, look up – crowning the top of the museum is the artist's eye-catching wire sculpture *Cloud and Chair* (1990). The collection of over 300 pieces covers Tàpies' whole range of work, including abstract pieces such as *Grey Ochre on Brown* (1962). Temporary exhibitions are also held here, with past shows by Mario Herz and Hans Hacke.

6 Els Encants
📍 H3 📍 Av Meridiana 69 🕐 9am–8pm Mon, Wed, Fri & Sat 🌐 encantsbarcelona.com

For almost a hundred years, the Els Encants market was a rambling, chaotic jumble of street stalls. In 2014, it got a striking new home and now its numerous stalls are arranged in a gentle upward spiral under a mirrored canopy designed to keep off the sun. As well as antiques, curiosities and other general bric-a-brac, you'll find textiles, household goods, records and vintage clothes here.

The modern glass exterior of *Museu del Disseny de Barcelona*

7 Casa de les Punxes (Casa Terradas)
📍 F2 📍 Av Diagonal 416 🌐 casa-lespunxes.com

This Gothic-style castle with four towers was designed by Modernista architect Josep Puig i Cadafalch and finished in 1905 for the Terradas sisters who owned several buildings on this street. It has always housed private homes, and today it also contains a co-working space. From the outside you can admire the ironwork on the balconies, the carved reliefs and the stained-glass windows. The ceramic panels mounted on the façade represent the patriotic symbols of Catalonia.

8 Rambla de Catalunya
📍 E2

This extension of the better-known Rambla is a more upmarket version of it. Lined with trees that form a leafy green tunnel in summer, it features scores of pretty façades and shops, including the Modernista Farmàcia Bolos (No. 77). The busy avenue teems with terrace bars and cafés.

9 Museu Egipci
📍 E2 📍 C/València 284 🕐 10am–2pm & 4–7:30pm Mon–Sat, 10am–2pm Sun 🌐 museuegipci.com 📱

Spain's most important Egyptology museum houses more than 350 exhibits from over 3,000 years of Ancient Egyptian history. Exhibits

ILDEFONS CERDÀ

Ildefons Cerdà's design for Eixample, the new part of the city, comprising a uniform grid of square blocks, received backing in 1859. Reflecting Cerdà's utopian socialist ideals, each block was to have a garden-like courtyard surrounded by uniform flats. Real estate vultures soon intervened, though, and the courtyards were converted into warehouses and factories. Today these green spaces are gradually being reinstated.

include terracotta figures, human and animal mummies, and a bust of the goddess Sekhmet (700–300 BCE).

10 Museu del Disseny de Barcelona

📍 H3 🏛 Pl de la Glòries Catalanes 37–38 🕐 3:30–9pm Mon, 9am–9pm Tue– Sun) 🌐 ajuntament.barcelona. cat/museudeldisseny

A monolithic hulk hosts this museum showcasing architecture, fashion and graphic design. The glass-and-zinc-clad building is a design statement in its own right. It also houses two leading independent, non-profit associations promoting design and architecture, the Foment de les Arts i del Disseny (FAD) and Barcelona Centre de Disseny (BCD).

THE MODERNISTA ROUTE

Morning

Visit the **Museu del Modernisme de Barcelona** (C/Balmes 48, www. mmbcn.cat) for an introduction to Catalan Art Nouveau via a series of exhibitions, then stroll around the gardens of the university. Head east along Gran Via past the **El Palace Barcelona Hotel** (p146) and turn right down C/Bruc and right again onto C/Casp for a glimpse of Gaudí's **Casa Calvet**. Walk two blocks west to the Pg de Gràcia; then go right again three blocks to the **Mansana de la Discòrdia** (p111) and explore **Casa Lleó Morera**, **Casa Amatller** or **Casa Batlló** – or all three (p50) if you have the time. Sniff around the **Museu del Perfum** and **Regia** perfume shop (p49) before continuing north to marvel at Gaudí's **La Pedrera** (p34). Take a lunch break at **Windsor** (p117)

Afternoon

After lunch, return to Pg de Gràcia then turn right along Av Diagonal, taking in the **Casa de les Punxes** at No. 416. Continue on Diagonal, turning left at Pg Sant Joan to see the Modernista Palau Macaya, now the CaixaForum Macaya cultural centre at No. 100. Then stroll along C/Mallorca to the **Sagrada Família** (p22). Here you can take in the Nativity Façade in the Plaça de Gaudí before climbing the bell towers for a view of the city.

Design Shops

A dazzling display of home accessories at Pilma

1. Pilma
E1 Av Diagonal 403 Sun
pilma.com
This shop sells modern furniture and decor items made by big names, as well as cutting-edge creations by a range of Catalan designers.

2. DomésticoShop
D1 Av Diagonal 419 Sun
domesticoshop.com
A household name in the interior design world, this split-level shop has furniture, domestic knick-knacks and a cute café.

3. Regia
E2 Pg de Gràcia 39 Sun
regia.es
The biggest perfume shop in the city has over 1,000 scents to choose from, including all the leading brands, and smaller makers. The space also plays host to the Museu del Perfum (p49).

4. Dos i Una
E2 C/Roselló 275 dosi unabarcelona.com
This designer gift shop sells "made in Barcelona" items and souvenirs.

5. Odd Kiosk
D2 C/València 222
oddkiosk.com
Barcelona's first LGBTQ+ news kiosk is slick and packed with style magazines, fanzines and cards.

6. Nanimarquina
F2 Rosselló 256 Sun & Mon
nanimarquina.com
Exquisite handmade carpets and textiles are sold in this artful shop.

7. Azul Tierra
E1 C/Còrsega 276–282
Sun & Mon azultierra.es
A huge, warehouse-style space with gorgeous furniture, Azul Tierra also sells lighting and all kinds of decorative objects ranging from mirrors to candles.

8. Àmbit
F2 C/Aragó 338 ambit barcelona.com
This huge showroom has a wide range of furniture from top designers, plus a selection of kilims, carpets, cushions, mirrors and other decorative objects.

9. Nordik Think
D1 C/Casanova 214 Sun
en.nordicthink.com/showroom
For the best in Scandinavian design, head to Nordik Think. On offer here are minimalist furnishings, lighting, decorative objects and much more by top designers from northern Europe.

10. Bagués Joieria
E2 Pg de Gràcia 41 Sun
bagues-masriera.com
Every piece at this jewellery shop is handmade using traditional methods.

Elegant contemporary furniture at Nordik Think

Bars

1. Sips
D2 C/Muntaner 108 6:30pm–2am Tue–Sat sips.barcelona

The best bar in the world, according to World's Best Bars 2023, this is where you'll find extraordinary cocktails. For an even more elevated experience, try their cocktail tasting menu: Esencia.

2. Xixbar
C4 C/Rocafort 19 Hours vary, check website xixbar.net

A highly reputed bar, Xixbar is known for its gin and tonics. The city's best spirits are sold in the shop next door.

3. Les Gens Que J'Aime
E2 C/València 286 6pm–2:30am Mon–Thu & Sun, 7pm–3am Fri & Sat lesgensquejaime.com

A basement cocktail bar, Les Gens Que J'Aime is the perfect spot for a drink and great lounge music.

4. Slow Bar
D1 C/París 186 93 368 14 55 7pm–5am Mon–Fri, 6pm–6am Sat (club: Fri & Sat only)

This red-hued bar also has a club and live music venue. It offers a range of cocktails which you can sample.

5. Bar Marfil
E2 Rambla de Catalunya 104 8am–midnight daily slowbar-celona.es

Located inside Hotel Murmuri, this is a trendy bar on a fancy shopping street. Sink into a plush faux-Baroque armchair and sip a cocktail.

6. Cotton House Hotel Terrace
F3 Gran Via de les Corts Catalanes 670 93 450 50 45 7am–midnight daily

A jungle of plants, wicker furnishings and fabulous cocktails make this chic hotel terrace bar the perfect place to enjoy a drink.

7. Ideal
D2 C/Aribau 89 93 453 10 28 Noon–2am daily (to 2:30am Fri & Sat)

Opened by legendary barman José María Gotarda in 1931, this place offers more than 80 kinds of whisky.

8. Jardin del Alma
E2 C/Mallorca 271 93 216 44 78 5–9pm daily

Set in the chic Alma Barcelona hotel this enchanting secret garden is the perfect place for a glass of wine and some tapas dishes.

9. Solange
D1 C/Aribau 143 6pm–1:30am daily (to 2:30am Fri & Sat) solangecocktail.com

This swanky cocktail bar has a James Bond-themed menu and expert mixologists.

10. Dry Martini
D1 C/Aribau 162 hours vary, check website drymartiniorg.com

An elegant venue to enjoy cocktails prepared by talented bartenders, while jazz plays in the background.

A cosy nook at the old-school cocktail bar Dry Martini

Exposed brick walls and wooden accents inside Oma Bistro

Cafés

1. Laie Llibreria Cafè
🅟 E3 🄰 C/Pau Claris 85 📞 93 318 17 39 🄲 Sun

A cultural meeting place with a lively atmosphere, airy terrace and one of the best bookshops in town. There's an excellent set lunch.

2. Cafè del Centre
🅟 F3 🄰 C/Girona 69 🄲 Sun & Mon 🅦 cafedelcentre.com

Said to be the oldest café in Eixample, this has been elegantly remodelled but retains its original dark wooden furnishings. It's great for a coffee break and the set lunch menu is excellent too.

3. Casa Alfonso
🅟 F3 🄰 C/Roger de Llúria 6 🄲 Sun 🅦 casaalfonso.com

This classy spot has been in business since 1929. It offers arguably the best *pernil* (serrano ham) in the city.

4. Oma Bistro
🅟 D3 🄰 C/Consell de Cent 227 🅦 omabarcelona.com

Set in a welcoming loft-style space, Oma Bistro is a local favourite. It is known for its superb brunch.

5. Pastelerias Mauri
🅟 E2 🄰 Rambla Catalunya 102 🄲 Sun D 🅦 pasteleriasmauri.com

First opened in 1929, this continues to be one of the best pastry shops in town. Enjoy a hot drink with a tasty dessert.

6. The Coffee House
🅟 D2 🄰 C/València 143 📞 63 105 08 36 🄲 8am–8pm Mon–Fri, 9am– 2pm Sat & Sun

Tuck into hearty breakfasts, brunches and homemade cakes with excellent coffee at this pretty café.

7. Baluard
🅟 F2 🄰 Praktik Bakery Hotel, C/ Provença 279 📞 93 269 48 18 🄲 Sun D

Located inside the lobby of a Scandinavian-style urban hotel, this café-bakery offers gourmet salads, sandwiches and pastries.

8. Velódromo
🅟 D1 🄰 C/Muntaner 213 🅦 barvelodromo.com

A historic bar with original 1930s furnishings, Velódromo was reopened by celebrity chef Carles Abellan. The menu features Catalan classics.

9. Manso's Café
🅟 C4 🄰 C/Manso 1 📞 93 348 63 46

Enjoy fabulous homemade cakes, coffee (with a choice of milks), soups and quiches at this café. Eat out on the little terrace or in the cosy interior.

10. Granja Petitbo
🅟 D2 🄰 C/Mallorca 194 🅦 granjapetitbo.com

Sink into a sofa and tuck into light meals at this café. Plenty of vegan and vegetarian options are available.

Restaurants and Tapas Bars

1. Joséphine

🅿 E2 🏠 C/Pau Claris 147 📞 93 853
55 40 · €

Coffee and snacks are served all day at
this French-themed café. There's also
an evening menu.

2. Cinc Sentits

🅿 D2 🏠 C/Aribau 58 🕐 Mon–Wed
🌐 cincsentits.com · €€€

Indulge the five senses (*cinc sentits* in
Catalan) at this restaurant where the
chef's modern take on classic Catalan
cuisine has won it two Michelin stars.

3. Igueldo

🅿 E2 🏠 C/Rosselló 186 🕐 Sun
🌐 restauranteigueldo.com · €€

Updated Basque cuisine is served in
elegant surroundings here.

4. Disfrutar

🅿 D2 🏠 Carrer de Villarroel, 163 🕐 Mon
& Sun 🌐 disfrutarbarcelona.com · €€€

Located in front of Ninot market,
Disfrutar lets you feast on avant-
garde dishes that offer a complete
gastronomic experience.

5. Casa Carmen

🅿 E3 🏠 C/Casp 17 📞 93 412 57 97
🕐 Hours vary, call ahead · €€

This is part of a small chain that
combines elegant decor with traditional
Spanish cuisine at affordable prices.

6. Cervecería Catalana

🅿 E2 🏠 C/Mallorca 236
📞 93 216 03 68 · €

Close to the Rambla de Catalunya,
this spot serves some of the best
tapas in town with a variety of beers.

7. Windsor

🅿 E1 🏠 C/Còrsega 286 🕐 3 weeks in
Aug 🌐 restaurantwindsor.com · €€€

Catalan *haute cuisine* is served
in elegant surroundings with
chandeliers and red upholstered
furniture. There's also a garden
for alfresco dining.

8. La Taverna del Clínic

🅿 D2 🏠 C/Rosselló 155 🕐 Sun
🌐 latavernadelclinic.com · €€

This smart, sophisticated tapas
bar serves some of the most
creative food in the city.

9. Paco Meralgo

🅿 D1 🏠 C/Muntaner 171 🌐 restaurant-
pacomeralgo.com · €

A bright, stylish tapas bar, Paco
Meralgo has a gourmet menu based
on recipes from around the country.

10. Moments

🅿 E3 🏠 Pg de Gràcia 38–40 📞 93 151
87 81 🕐 Tue–Sat D & Sat L · €€€

Set in the ultra-luxurious Mandarin
Oriental (*p146*), Moments has been
awarded two Michelin stars for its
sublime renditions of Catalan classics,
from langoustine tartare to scallops
with artichokes. Tastings and à la
carte and menus are offered.

**The plush dining room of Moments
at the Mandarin Oriental**

GRÀCIA, TIBIDABO AND ZONA ALTA

The hilly Zona Alta covers several neighbourhoods, from the moneyed Pedralbes and hilly Tibidabo to vibrant Gràcia. The area offers stunning views and regal attractions, but what sets it apart are its 15 parks – the best are Collserola, spread like green baize over Tibidabo mountain, and Gaudí's Park Güell. The charming Tibidabo is crowned by the striking Temple Expiatori del Sagrat Cor (Church of the Sacred Heart). Cosmopolitan Gràcia's political tradition and Roma community have long drawn artists and writers to its labyrinthine streets, and its squares are now home to lively bars and stores.

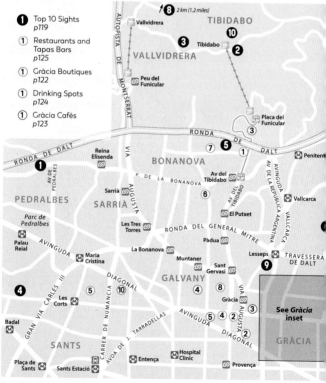

For places to stay in this area, see p147

1 Monestir de Pedralbes

🚉 B1 🏛 C/Baixada del Monestir
🕐 From 10am Tue–Sun; closing
hours vary, chech website
🌐 monestirpedralbes.barcelona 🔗

Named after the Latin *petras albas*,
which means "white stones", this
outstandingly beautiful Gothic
monastery was founded by Queen
Elisenda de Montcada de Piños in
1327 with the support of her husband,
James II of Aragón. Her alabaster tomb
lies in the wall between the church and
the impressive three-storey Gothic
cloister. The furnished kitchens, cells,
infirmary and refectory, which are
all very well preserved, provide an
interesting glimpse into what medieval
life was like.

A traditional carousel at Parc
d'Atraccions del Tibidabo

2 Parc d'Atraccions del Tibidabo

🚉 B1 🏛 Pl de Tibidabo 🕐 Hours
vary, chech website 🌐 tibidabo.
cat 🔗

Take the funicular up to the top
of Tibidabo's 517-m (1,695-ft)
mountain to visit this traditional
amusement park, which opened
in 1908. There are a couple of white-
knuckle rides, but the real attractions
are the old-fashioned ones, including
a beautifully pre-served carousel and
a Ferris wheel. There's also the fabulous
Museu dels Autòmates *(p49)*, with automatons, mechanical models and
a scale model of the park.

3 Torre de Collserola

🚉 B1 🏛 Parc de Collserola
🕐 Until further notice 🌐 torre
decollserola.com

This slender telecommunications
tower was designed by British architect
Sir Norman Foster, opening in time
for the Barcelona Olympic Games in
summer 1992. The needle-like upper
structure rests on a concrete pillar,
anchored by 12 huge steel cables,
rising to a height of 288 m (945 ft).
The top can be reached by a glass-
fronted lift and on a clear day, you
can see as far as Montserrat and
the Pyrenees.

Camp Nou, Europe's biggest stadium and home to FC Barcelona

4 FC Barcelona Museum and Stadium Tour

A2 **Av Arístides Maillol** **Hours vary, chech website; advance booking recommended** **fcbarcelona.com**

The Museu del FC Barcelona, the city's most visited museum, is a must for the fans. Its location has moved while the famous Camp Nou stadium is being rebuilt (slated for completion 2026), but the temporary venue still features lots of interactive exhibits, memorabilia and, of course, the famous trophy display.

5 CosmoCaixa Museu de la Ciència

B1 **C/Isaac Newton 26** **10am–8pm daily** **cosmocaixa.org/es/museo-ciencia-barcelona**

Barcelona's science museum is a thoroughly stimulating and interactive affair. It occupies a glass-and-steel building, with six of its nine storeys set underground. Displays include a wide range of historic objects, flora and fauna. One of its most important pieces is a recreated section of flooded Amazon rainforest, which includes fish, reptiles, mammals, birds and plants from the region. A tour through Earth's geological history explains processes such as erosion and sedimentation. There are also innovative temporary exhibitions that cover environmental issues.

6 Park Güell

A UNESCO World Heritage Site, this heady brew of architectural wizardry (p32) includes *trencadís* tiling, fairy-tale pavilions, Gothic archways and the columned Sala Hipóstila (originally designed as a market hall). In true Gaudí style, playfulness and symbolism pervade every aspect of the park. The Casa-Museu Gaudí, where Gaudí lived for 20 years, is dedicated to his life.

7 Parc del Laberint d'Horta

C1 **C/German Desvalls** **10am–dush daily**

In 1802, the Marquès d'Alfarràs hosted a huge party in these wonderful Neo-Classical gardens in honour of Charles I. Designed by Italian architect Domenico Bagutti, they feature elegant pavilions, a lake, a waterfall, canals and a cypress-tree hedge maze. The gardens are closed in November.

GRÀCIA

Until the late 19th century, Gràcia was a fiercely independent city. Despite locals' protests, it became part of Barcelona in 1898, but has maintained a sense of separatism and has been a hotbed of political activity. It is home to a cottage industry of crafts, nurtured by a growing band of artisans. Do not miss the *barri's* annual fiesta (p74) in the second week of August.

The Temple Expiatori del Sagrat Co crowned by a huge statue of Jesu

8 Parc de Collserola

B1 **C/Església 92**
parcnaturalcollserola.cat

Beyond the peaks of Tibidabo mountain, this 6,500-ha (16,000-acre) natural park of wild forest and winding paths is an oasis of calm. It is great for hiking and biking, with signposted paths and nature trails.

9 Casa Vicens

E1 **Carrer de les Carolines 20** **Apr–Oct: 10am–8pm daily; Nov–Mar: 10am–7pm daily (to 3pm Mon)** **casavicens.org**

Gaudí's first major commission, this former private home is situated on a quiet residential street. It was once surrounded by orchards and fields, a fact the architect has referenced on the façade; a patchwork of tiles decorated with marigolds. Inside, rooms are replete with florid marquetry, arabesque detailing and nature-inspired ambiances.

10 Temple Expiatori del Sagrat Cor

The Neo-Gothic Temple of the Sacred Heart (p46) was built by Enric Sagnier between 1902 and 1911. It has a dramatic sculpture of Jesus and an elaborate door. Take the elevator up the main tower, or climb up to the outside terrace for great views.

EXPLORING THE HEIGHTS

Morning

Taking the northern route of the Bus Turístic is the easiest way to negotiate the northern area of Barcelona; it also gives discounts on entrance to major sights en route. Start off at **Plaça de Catalunya** (p52) – tickets can be bought on board – and sit on the top deck for a good view of the Modernista magic along Pg de Gràcia. Make the whimsical **Park Güell** your first stop and spend the morning ambling around Gaudí's otherworldly park. Get back on the bus and continue north to the southern end of Av Tibidabo. Walk about 500 m (1,600 ft) up Av Tibidabo and stop off for a lunch in the garden of the **El Asador d'Aranda** (p125).

Afternoon

After you've had your fill of fine Castilian cuisine, stroll up Av Tibidabo to Plaça Doctor Andreu, where you can hop on the funicular train to go higher still to Plaça de Tibidabo. Pop into the **Parc d'Atraccions** (p119) for a ride on the dodgems or the Ferris wheel. Then head over to the landmark **Torre de Collserola** (p119). Return to Pl Doctor Andreu on the funicular and treat yourself to a granissat in one of the terrace bars. Catch the number 196 bus down the Av Tibidabo, then take Bus Turístic back to the city centre.

Gràcia Boutiques

Contemporary men's fashion at trendy concept store Boo

1. Boo
E1 C/Bonavista 2 93 368 14 58
11am–8:30pm Mon–Sat

An elegantly decorated space, Boo offers contemporary men's clothing and accessories with a vintage feel. International labels like Saint James, Norse Projects and tailored shirts by Tuk Tuk are available. There's also a selection of books and colognes.

2. Lydia Delgado
E1 C/Sèneca 28 93 218 16 30 Noon–8pm Mon–Fri, 11am–2pm Sat

This well-established Catalan designer creates clothing for women inspired by the 1950s and 1960s. Touches of embroidery, patchwork and other details enliven the fabrics.

3. José Rivero
F1 C/Astúries 43 93 237 33 88
11am–2pm & 5–9pm Mon–Sat

José provides his own original in-house creations for women; he also sells accessories by young, local designers.

4. Berta Sumpsi
F1 C/Verdi 98 676 870 122
11am–2pm & 5–8pm Mon–Sat

This space doubles as a workshop and showroom. There is a wide range of simple, sculptural jewellery displayed in minimal surroundings.

5. Érase Una Vez
E1 C/Bonavista 13 697 805 409
10:30am–2pm & 5–8pm Mon–Fri, 11am–2pm Sat

Literally translating to "once upon a time", this shop creates unique wedding gowns. It also stocks some of the most exclusive designers.

6. Nana Banana
F1 C/ Verdi 24 93 311 21 14
11am–9pm Mon–Sat

The vibe of Gràcia is captured in this boutique that stocks creations of young, local designers. The clothes here range from bright overalls to graphic T-shirts.

7. Picnic
F1 C/Verdi 17 93 016 63 53

One of several chic little boutiques on C/Verdi, Picnic has a carefully curated selection of women's fashion and accessories from local labels.

8. Mushi Mushi
F1 C/Bonavista 12 93 292 29 74 11am–2:30pm & 4:30–8:30pm Mon–Sat

From hard-to-find small labels to the best international collections, Mushi Mushi stocks an impressive selection of women's fashion and accessories.

9. El Piano
F1 C/Verdi 20 bis 93 415 51 76
11am–2:30pm & 4:30–8:30pm Mon–Fri, 11am–9pm Mon–Sat

This store sells womenswear with a retro flair made by Catalan designer Tina García. It also stocks clothes by other independent designers.

10. Botó and Co
E1 C/Bonavista 3 93 676 22 71
10:30am–8:30pm Mon–Sat

A multibrand store, Botó and Co sells stylish high-quality women's fashion, including Current/Elliot jeans, Humanoid sweaters and more.

Gràcia Cafés

Cafè del Sol
F1 Pl del Sol 16 93 237 14 48
This café-bar is a cut above the others in the lively Plaça del Sol. The atmosphere buzzes, the conversation inspires and the excellent coffee keeps on coming.

Cafè Salambó
F1 C/Torrijos 51 93 218 69 66
Scrumptious sandwiches and salads are the draw at this bar and café. There are pool tables upstairs.

Bar Quimet
E1 C/Vic 23 93 218 41 89
An old-fashioned bar with big wooden barrels and marble-topped tables, this is a great spot for an aperitif. Try the *vermut* (vermouth) and a selection of olives and *boquerones* (fresh anchovies).

La Cafetera
F1 Pl de la Virreina 2
lacafeterabar.com
Of all the cafés on Plaça de la Virreina, La Cafetera, with its outdoor terrace and tiny patio full of potted plants, is perhaps one of the nicest options for a quiet and leisurely morning coffee and a sandwich or pastry.

5. Suís & Bowls
E1 Travessera de Gràcia 151
elsuis.com
Healthy meals and fresh salads are the specialities at this colourful café. Additionally, fresh juices, cakes and pastries are also on offer.

6. Mama's Café
F1 C/Torrijos 26 93 210 00 50
Tue
A pretty minimalist spot with a small patio at the back, Mama's Café serves organic sandwiches, salads and homemade cakes all day. Don't forget to try the fresh fruit juices and cocktails.

7. Bicioci Bike Café
F1 C/Venus 1 93 458 20 44
Dedicated to bike lovers, Bicioci's decor features bikes hanging from the ceiling. Here you will find excellent coffee, cakes, brunches and daily lunch specials.

8. Cafè del Teatre
F1 C/Torrijos 41 93 416 06 51
This is a great place to find a young, friendly crowd and good conversation. The only connection with the theatre, however, seems to be the velvet curtains on the sign over the door of this scruffy yet popular café.

9. La Nena
F1 C/Ramón y Cajal 36
93 285 14 76
The room with tables and games for children here makes this a popular choice with parents of young kids. The range of homemade cakes, juices and hot drinks on offer are a neighbourhood favourite.

10. Sabio Infante
F1 C/Torrent de l'Olla 39
Mon sabioinfante.com
Sample tasty homemade cakes and great coffee at Sabio Infante. The interior is decorated with all sorts of weird and wonderful kitsch finds.

The busy Plaça de la Virreina, lined with pretty outdoor cafés

Drinking Spots

1. Bobby Gin
E1 C/Francisco Giner 47
bobbygin.com
This cocktail bar stocks some
60 premium gins – floral, citric,
spiced and vintage. Their slogan,
"Respect the gin", comes courtesy
of the eponymous bartender.

2. Las Vermudas
F1 C/Robí 32 Mon las
vermudas.com
Vermut (vermouth) shows no signs of
losing popularity, and Las Vermudas
features a fantastic selection of it.
Enjoy a glass out on the terrace, or
at one of the live concerts.

3. Mirablau
Pl Dr Andreu mirablaubcn.cat
A slightly older, well-heeled set who
adhere to the smart dress code come
to this bar for a combination of
cocktails and views of the city.

4. Gimlet
D1 C/Santaló 46 Sun dry
martiniorg.com
Opened in 1982 by the renowned
mixologist Javier de las Muelas, Gimlet
is a classic bar with contemporary flair,
where you can enjoy premium drinks
in elegant surroundings.

5. Luz de Gas
D1 C/Muntaner 246 Sun–Tue
luzdegas.com
A major player since the mid-1990s,
this former theatre retains its retro
charm with red velvet drapes and
chandeliers. It now features live
bands and DJs.

6. El Tresss Bar
F1 C/Alzina 2 34 934 06 98 32
Tucked away behind the Plaça
de la Virreina, this friendly spot is
furnished with vintage finds. It has
a cosy atmosphere and a pretty
terrace – ideal for relaxing.

7. Torre Rosa
C/Francesc Tàrrega 22 L daily
torrerosa.com
This neighbourhood favourite is ideal
for escaping the summer heat, with
tables scattered under a cluster of
palm trees. There is a wide range of
cocktails on offer.

8. La Cervesera Artesana
F1 C/Sant Agustí 14
A friendly microbrewery, this spot
serves a good range of imported beer
in addition to their own excellent
brews. The Iberian Pale Ale, a mellow
amber beer, is certainly worth a try.

9. Elephanta
F1 Torrent d'en Vidalet, 37
elephanta.cat
Specializing in flavoured gins, Elephant
also offers fine cocktails, served in an
intimate space. The bar doubles as a
mellow café during early evenings.

10. Bikini
C1 Av Diagonal 547 Mon & Tue
bikinibcn.com
Open from midnight, this huge venue
has three spaces, offering dance and
Latin music and a cocktail lounge.
Regular live music includes some of
the best acts in Europe.

**Bottles lining the shelves behind
the bar at Bobby Gin**

Restaurants and Tapas Bars

Vintage decor at the convivial Bonanova restaurant

appeal while serving excellent food. Gourmet tapas and cocktails are served in the lovely garden at the back.

El Asador d'Aranda
Av Tibidabo 31 93 417 01 15 · €€
Set in the Modernista Casa Roviralta, this restaurant is a magnet for business-people. Order the delicious lamb roasted in an oak-burning oven and dine in the beautiful garden.

2. Hofmann
E1 C/La Granada del Penedès 14–16 Sat L, Sun, Easter Wk, Aug, Christmas hofmann-bcn.com · €€€
Established by the late chef Mey Hofmann, this Michelin-starred spot serves exceptional Catalan cuisine. Save room for the desserts.

Abissínia
F1 C/Torrent de les Flors 55
93 213 07 85 Tue · €
Tasty Ethiopian stews are served with injera bread (flatbread) here. This is a good restaurant for vegetarians.

Il Giardinetto
E1 C/La Granada del Penedès 28
Sat L, Sun ilgiardinetto.es · €€
This restaurant features whimsical, garden-themed decor and serves classic Mediterranean dishes with a twist such as spaghetti alla Sofia Loren (pasta served with anchovy and parsley sauce).

Fragments Café
Pl de la Concòrdia 12 93 419 96 13
Mon · €€
Plaça de la Concòrdia, in the Les Corts neighbourhood, retains a small-town

6. Bonanova
C/Sant Gervasi de Cassoles 103
93 417 10 33 Sun D, Mon · €€
Away from the tourist routes, Bonanova has been serving fresh, seasonal fare cooked in a simple and traditional way since 1964.

7. La Balsa
C/Infanta Isabel 4 Sun D, Easter, Aug L labalsarestaurant.com · €€
With two garden terraces, La Balsa is a beautiful spot in the Bonanova area, serving fine Basque, Catalan and Mediterranean dishes.

8. Pappa e Citti
E1 C/Moliné 11 687 657 111
Sun · €
This place has wonderful Sardinian dishes prepared with fresh ingredients. Try the platter of breads, cheeses, cured meats or the stews or pastas.

9. Bar Vall
F1 Plaça Rovira i Trias 93 213 34 24 · €
Set in one of Gràcia's prettiest squares, Bar Vall serves sandwiches, salads and tapas, as well as more substantial meals.

10. Botafumeiro
E1 C/Gran de Gràcia 81
botafumeiro.es/en/home · €€€
The fish tanks here teem with crabs and lobsters destined for dinner plates. Try the pulpo Gallego (Galician octopus). Be sure to book ahead.

BEYOND BARCELONA

Steeped in tradition, with its own language and pride in its identity, Catalonia is rich in both cultural heritage and physical beauty. It is not hyperbole to say that Catalonia has everything. The coastline has beautiful sandy beaches, intimate rocky coves and clear waters, while to the north are the 3,000-m (10,000-ft) Pyrenean peaks. These natural treasures are complemented by fabulous churches and monasteries in stunning mountain settings. The cuisine is rewarding, while the local cava holds its own against its French champagne counterparts.

For places to stay in this area, see p147

The Montserrat mountain towering behind the Monestir de Montserrat

1 Montserrat

🛈 Pl de la Creu; montserratvisita.com

The dramatic Montserrat mountain, with its remote Benedictine monastery (dating from 1025), is a religious symbol and a place of pilgrimage for the Catalan people. The basilica houses a statue of the patron saint of Catalonia, La Moreneta, also known as the "Black Virgin" (p47). Some legends date the statue to 50 CE, but research suggests it was carved in the 12th century. The monastery was largely destroyed in 1811, during the War of Independence, and exquisitely rebuilt some 30 years later. Montserrat – Catalan for "jagged mountain" – forms part of a ridge that rises suddenly from the plains. Take the funicular up to the peaks, where paths run alongside spectacular gorges to numerous hermitages.

2 Teatre-Museu Dalí, Figueres

🏛 Teatre-Museu Dalí: Pl Gala-Salvador Dalí, Figueres 🕐 Hours vary, chech website 🌐 salvador-dali.org 🌀

Salvador Dalí was born in the town of Figueres in 1904. Paying tribute to the artist is the Teatre-Museu Dalí, which is filled with his eccentric works. Housed in a former theatre, the country's second-most-visited museum (after the Prado in Madrid) provides a unique insight into the artist's creations, from La Cesta de Pan (1926) to El Torero Alucinógeno (1970). A 30-minute drive away, close to the beach town of Cadaqués, the Dalí connection continues. Here, you can visit the Casa-Museu Salvador Dalí (Platja de, Portlligat), which was the artist's summer home for nearly 60 years until his death in 1989. These two sights are the main attractions of the "Dalí triangle". The third sight that completes this triangle is the Gala Dalí Castle House-Museum (Gala Dali, s/n, Púbol) located in Púbol, which was his gift to his wife, Gala.

Boats at the marina of Cadaqués, a picture-perfect beach town

3 Costa Brava

The Costa Brava is a beautiful stretch of Mediterranean coastline, which runs from Blanes, about 60 km (37 miles) north of Barcelona, all the way to the French border. There are a few big resorts, including Lloret de Mar and Roses, but many of the towns and resorts here, such as Calella de Palafrugell and Tamariu, have remained refreshingly low-key. Cultural highlights include the medieval citadel that crowns Tossa de Mar, and the Thyssen Museum in Sant Feliu de Guíxols. The area also has some excellent seafront hiking paths, such as the Camins de Ronda.

4 Alt Penedès

🛈 C/Hermengild Ciascar 2, Vilafranca del Penedès; penedsturisme.cat

Catalonia's most famous wine region is the *cava*-producing area of the Penedès. The *cava* brands of Cordoníu and Freixenet have become household names worldwide. Many of the area's wineries and bodegas are open to the public. Cordoníu's is one of the most spectacular, housed in a Modernista building designed by Puig i Cadafalch, with cellars spread across a phenomenal 26 km (16 miles) over five floors.

5 Begur and around

🛈 Av Onze de Setembre 5; visitbegur.cat

The elegant hilltop town of Begur, with its ruined 14th-century castle, looks down over pristine wetlands and some of the prettiest coves on the Costa Brava. The town's population quadruples in summer as visitors make this their base for exploring nearby beaches and small, isolated coves. Many of the area's beaches stage jazz concerts during the summer. This is perhaps the best stretch of coast-line in Catalonia.

6 Tarragona

🛈 C/Major 39; tarragona turisme.cat

The city of Tarragona was once the capital of Roman Catalonia, and its main attractions are from this era. Various archaeological treasures include an impressive amphitheatre and well-preserved Roman walls that lead past the Museu Nacional Arqueològic (currently closed for restoration) and the Torre de Pilatos, where Christians were supposedly imprisoned before being thrown to the lions. The Catedral de Santa Tecla *(p130)* is also in Tarragona.

7 Girona

🛈 Rambla de la Llibertat 1; girona.cat/turisme

Girona is a beautiful little town surrounded by lush green hills. Hidden away in the old town, the atmospheric Jewish quarter, known as El Call, is one of Europe's best-preserved medieval enclaves. Visiting Girona's cathedral *(p130)* is a must.

8 Empúries

🛈 C/Puig i Cadafalch s/n, Empúries ⏱10am–5pm (Jun–Sep: to 8pm; Oct–mid-Nov & mid-Feb–May: to 6pm) 🌐 mac empuries.cat 🔗

After Tarragona, Empúries is Catalonia's second most important

Roman site. Located by the sea, it is spread across more than 40 ha (99 acres) of land scattered with Greek and Roman ruins, the highlights of which are the remains of a market street, various temples and a Roman amphitheatre. It's an ideal spot for those looking to mix a bit of history with a dip in the sea.

9 PortAventura World

📍 Av Pere Molas, Vila-seca, Tarragona 🕐 Hours vary, chech website 🌐 portaventuraworld.com 🔁

This theme park is divided into six areas, including the Far West and Polynesia, and has some of Europe's biggest rollercoasters, as well as a thrilling Ferrari Land.

10 Costa Daurada and Sitges

📍 Pl Eduard Maristany 2, Sitges; visitsitges.com

With its sandy beaches and shallow waters, the Costa Daurada is a prime attraction. Torredembarra is a family resort, but the crown jewel is Sitges, the summer home to Barcelona's chic crowd, and a popular destination for LGBTQ+ travellers. Restaurants and bars line Sitges' main boulevard, the Passeig Marítim, while Modernista architecture is scattered among the 1970s blocks.

Surfers emerging from the sea on a pretty, sandy beach at Sitges

A SCENIC DRIVE

↑ from Barcelona 85 km (53 miles)

Morning

This drive should take about five hours for a round trip. From Barcelona take the AP7 motorway until exit 4, then take the C260 to **Cadaqués**. Just before entering the town, stop at the viewpoint and take in the gorgeous view of this former fishing village. Once in Cadaqués, wander the charming boutique-filled streets of what is now one of Catalonia's trendiest beach towns. After a splash in the sea and a coffee at one of the chic terrace cafés, take the road leaving Port Lligat and head for the lighthouse on **Cap de Creus** (p131). Drive through the beautiful landscape of this rocky headland before doubling back and heading off to Port de la Selva. The road twists and winds interminably, but the picture-perfect scenery will leave you speechless.

Afternoon

Enjoy a seafood lunch at Ca l'Herminda (C/Illa 7), in the small, mountain-enclosed Port de la Selva. Then drive to the neighbouring village of Selva del Mar, with its tiny river, for a post-prandial coffee on the terrace of the Bar Stop (C/Port de la Selva 1), before continuing up to the **Monestir de Sant Pere de Rodes** (p130). You'll be tempted to stop frequently on the way up to take in the views. Don't, because the best is to be had from the monastery itself – a sweeping vista of the whole area. There are plenty of well-signposted walks around the mountain top, and it is worth sticking around to see the sun set slowly over the bay.

Churches and Monasteries

The superb vaulted ceiling of the Monestir de Montserrat's apse

1. Monestir de Montserrat

🅐 Montserrat 🅦 abadiamont serrat.cat 🖸

Catalonia's holiest place (p127) and its most visited monastery has splendid Romanesque art and a statue of the "Black Virgin".

2. Monestir de Poblet

🅐 Off N240, 10 km (6 miles) W of Montblanc 🅦 poblet.cat 🖸

This beautiful working monastery contains the Gothic Capella de Sant Jordi, a Romanesque church, and the Porta Daurada, a doorway that was gilded for Felipe II's visit in 1564.

3. Monestir de Ripoll

🅐 Ripoll 🅦 monestirderi poll.cat 🖸

The west portal of this monastery (879 CE) has reputedly the finest Romanesque carvings in Spain. Of the original buildings, only the doorway and cloister remain.

4. Monestir de Santes Creus

🅐 Santes Creus, 25 km (15 miles) NW of Montblanc 🅠 Mon 🅦 patri moni.gencat.cat/en/monuments 🖸

The cloister here (1150) is notable for the exquisitely sculpted capitals by English artist Reinard Fonoll. These capitals incorporate both English and Catalan design elements.

5. Sant Joan de les Abadesses

🅐 Sant Joan de les Abadesses 🅦 santjoandelesabadesses.cat 🖸

This monastery, established in the 9th century, houses an impressive Romanesque sculpture representing the Descent from the Cross.

6. Sant Climent i Santa Maria de Taüll

🅐 138 km (85 miles) N of Lleida 🅦 centreromanic.com

These two Romanesque churches, dating from 1123, are perfect examples of the ones that pepper the Pyrenees. The frescoes are reproductions of the originals, now housed in Barcelona's MNAC (p30).

7. Catedral de La Seu d'Urgell

🅐 La Seu d'Urgell 🅦 laseumedieval. com/en 🖸

Dating from around 1040, the Catedral de La Seu d'Urgell is one of the most elegant cathedrals in Catalonia.

8. Catedral de Girona

🅐 Plaça de la Catedral s/n, Girona 🅦 catedraldegirona.cat 🖸

This cathedral possesses the widest Gothic nave in Europe, after the basilica in the Vatican.

9. Catedral de Santa Tecla

🅐 Old Town, Tarragona 🅦 tarragonaturisme.cat 🖸 🖸

At 104 m (340 ft) long, Tarragona's cathedral is the largest in the region. Begun in the 12th century, it has an enchanting cloister.

10. Monestir de Sant Pere de Rodes

🅐 22 km (13 miles) E of Figueres 🅠 Mon 🅦 patrimoni.gencat.cat/en/ monuments 🖸

Perched on a hilltop, this medieval UNESCO World Heritage Site offers breathtaking views over Cap de Creus and Port de la Selva.

National Parks and Nature Reserves

1. Parc Nacional d'Aigüestortes i Estany de Sant Maurici
📍 148 km (90 miles) N of Lleida
🌐 parcsnaturals.gencat.cat/ca/xarxa-de-parcs

The magnificent peaks of Catalonia's only national park are accessible from the village of Espot. You'll discover beautiful waterfalls, lakes and glacial tarns 2,000 m (6,560 ft) up.

2. Delta de l'Ebre
📍 28 km (17 miles) SE of Tortosa
A patchwork of paddy fields, the wide expanse of the River Ebre is a nature reserve for migratory birds and has many birdwatching stations.

3. Parc Natural de la Zona Volcànica de la Garrotxa
📍 40 km (24 miles) NW of Girona
This natural park covers the volcanic area of La Garrotxa, which last erupted 10,000 years ago. The largest crater is the Santa Margalida, which is 500 m (1,640 ft) wide. It is best to visit in spring.

4. Cap de Creus
📍 36 km (22 miles) E of Figueres
The Pyrenees mountains form Catalonia's most easterly point offering great views of the coastline.

5. Parc Natural del Cadí-Moixeró
📍 20 km (12 miles) E of La Seu d'Urgell
Covered in a carpet of conifers and oaks, this mountain range has lush vegetation. Several of the peaks here are over 2,000 m (6,560 ft) high.

6. Parc Natural del Montseny
📍 48 km (30 miles) NW of Barcelona
🌐 parcs.diba.cat/es/web/montseny
Catalonia's most accessible natural park, these woodland hills are suitable for walkers and mountain bikers, with a vast network of trails. Take the popular climb up Turó de l'Home, the highest peak.

7. Massís de Pedraforca
📍 64 km (40 miles) N of Manresa
🌐 parcsnaturals.gencat.cat/ca/xarxa-de-parcs
A nature reserve surrounds this outcrop of mountains, a favourite of rock climbers.

8. Serra de l'Albera
📍 15 km (9 miles) N of Figueres
The Albera Massif is home to ancient dolmens, Romanesque sanctuaries and one of the last colonies of the Mediterranean tortoise.

9. Parc Natural dels Aiguamolls de l'Empordà
📍 15 km (9 miles) E of Figueres
This nature reserve hides a number of birdwatching towers. Those in the Laguna de Vilaüt and La Bassa de Gall Marí allow the observation of herons, moorhens and other bird species nesting in spring.

10. Parc Natural de Sant Llorenç del Munt
📍 12 km (7 miles) E of Manresa
🌐 parcs.diba.cat/web/santllorenc
Close to Barcelona, this park is home to large numbers of wild boar. Visit the Romanesque monastery at Cerro de la Mola, which is now a restaurant.

A purple heron with its catch at Delta de l'Ebre

Outdoor Activities

1. Rafting and Kayaking
One of Europe's best rivers for whitewater sports (*raftingpallars turisnat.com*) is La Noguera Pallaresa in the Pyrenees. Late spring is the best time to go, as the mountain snow begins to thaw.

2. Scuba Diving
The Illes Medes nature reserve is home to coral reefs and thousands of fish species. Glass-bottom boats (*barcanuria.com*) cater to non-divers while respecting the environment. Don't forget to bring reef-friendly sunscreen with you.

3. Watersports and Sailing
Good sailing can be found in Sitges (*clubmarsitges.com*), along with yachts for rent and classes for novices. Canoeing and windsurfing are also available.

4. Skiing
La Molina (*lamolina.cat*) is the most accessible Pyrenean ski resort from Barcelona, but the popular Baqueira-Beret (*baqueira.es*) is where the jet-set goes. Both offer all levels of skiing (including off-piste) from December onwards.

5. Golf
The Costa Brava is one of Europe's top golf destinations; the best courses are around Platja d'Aro (*97 281 67 27*) and Santa Cristina d'Aro (*97 283 70 55*).

6. Horse Riding
Montseny Natural Park (*p131*) is ideal for horse riding (*hipicacantramp.es*), with a number of stables.

7. Ballooning
A balloon journey (*voldecoloms.cat*) over the volcanic area of La Garrotxa is an unbeatable

Enjoying watersports in the azure waters at Castelldefels

way to get a bird's-eye view of the beautiful Catalonian landscape.

8. Boat Trips
Take a boat (*dofijetboats.com*) from Calella and Blanes along the Costa Brava, stopping at the old town and medieval castle of Tossa de Mar. Boats sail every hour daily from Blanes and Lloret de Mar, and twice daily from Calella. There are no boat trips between the months of October and March.

9. Activities at the Canal Olímpic
Originally used for rowing competitions in the Olympic Games in 1992, the magnificent Canal Olímpic (*canalolimpic.cat*) is now a leisure complex offering a host of activities.

10. Foraging for Mushrooms
From late September to late October, Catalans flock to the hills in search of *bolets* – wild mushrooms. Some are poisonous, so amateurs should make sure they get a guide through the Diputació de Barcelona (*diba.cat*).

Places to Eat

1. Tragamar

⌂ Passatge Jimmy Rena s/n, Calella de Palafrugell ☏ 97 261 43 36 ☒ Oct–Mar & Tue · €€

Book ahead for a table on the terrace or by one of the bay windows at this beachside restaurant, and enjoy stellar seafood dishes such as tuna carpaccio or lobster paella.

2. Les Cols

⌂ Mas les Cols, Ctra de la Canya s/n, Olot ☒ Sun D, Mon & Tue ⊞ lescols.com · €€€

Two-Michelin-starred Les Cols offers contemporary Spanish cuisine made with local seasonal produce in a stunning modern setting.

3. La Torre del Remei

⌂ Camí del Remei 3, Bolvir, Cerdanya ☒ Mon–Wed, Thu & Sun D · €€

A Modernista palace provides an elegant setting for wonderfully presented Catalan food.

4. Cal Ticus

⌂ C/Raval 19, Sant Sadurní d'Anoia ☒ D, Mon & Tue ⊞ ticusrestaurant.cat · €

This restaurant serves traditional cuisine using seasonal produce. A good selection of Penedès wines are on the list and for sale in their shop.

5. Fonda Europa

⌂ C/Anselm Clavé 1, Granollers ⊞ hotelfondaeuropa.com · €€

Established in 1771, Fonda Europa was the first in a line of successful Catalan restaurants. Specialities include pigs' trotters and a Catalan stockpot with meat and vegetables.

6. Lasal de Varador

⌂ Pg Marítim 1, Mataró ☏ 93 114 05 80 ☒ Dec–Feb · €€

This beachfront restaurant serves paellas, seafood and more, using organic and sustainably sourced ingredients.

7. Els Pescadors

⌂ Muelle Pesquero s/n, Arenys de Mar ☒ Sun ⊞ Delspescadors.com · €

Set inside the local *llotja* (wholesale fish market), this food spot serves fresh seafood. There are a few tables outside on the port overlooking the boats. Book ahead on the weekends.

8. Toc Al Mar

⌂ Pl d'Aiguablava, Begur ☒ Dec–Feb ⊞ tocalmar.cat · €

Located on a beach in Costa Brava, Toc Al Mar has tables on the sands. Sample freshly grilled seafood, such as Palamós prawns and Mediterranean delicacies.

9. El Celler de Can Roca

⌂ C/Can Sunyer 48, Girona ☒ Sun, Mon, Tue L ⊞ cellercanroca.com · €€€

The Roca brothers' exciting Catalan cuisine is complemented by great wines. The restaurant has three Michelin stars and an 11-month waiting list.

10. Cal Ton

⌂ C/Casal 8, Vilafranca del Penedès ☏ 93 890 37 41 ☒ Hours vary, call ahead · €€

Head to Cal Ton for contemporary cuisine in the heart of Catalonia's biggest wine region. Order the *menu degustació*.

Outdoor seating at the lovely Els Pescadors

STREETSMART

Bench tiles in Park Güell

GETTING AROUND

Whether exploring Barcelona by foot or making use of public transportation, here is everything you need to know to navigate the city and the surrounding areas like a pro.

AT A GLANCE

PUBLIC TRANSPORT COSTS

METRO

€2.40
Single-ride ticket

BUS

€2.40
Single-ride ticket

METRO, BUS, LOCAL TRAINS

€10.50
All-day travel ticket

SPEED LIMIT

MOTORWAY	DUAL CARRIAGEWAYS
120 km/h (75 mph)	**100** km/h (60 mph)

SECONDARY ROAD	URBAN AREAS
90 km/h (55 mph)	**50** km/h (30 mph)

Arriving by Air

Most flights arrive at **Josep Tarradella Barcelona-El Prat** Airport, Barcelona international airport, located 16 km (10 miles) west of the city. The airport has two terminals, linked by a shuttle bus. European budget airlines fly to Barcelona all year round and there are direct flights from several US hubs, including New York, Miami, Chicago, Washington DC and Atlanta. Flights from Australia and New Zealand transfer through Dubai and other stopovers. Regular internal flights operate between Madrid and Barcelona as well as to local airports: Lleida–Alguaire Airport, Reus Airport in Tarragona, Girona–Costa Brava Airport and Andorra–La Seu d'Urgell Airport. For information on getting to and from Barcelona's airport, see the table opposite.
Josep Tarradellas Barcelona-El Prat
W aena.es

International Train Travel

Spain's rail services are operated by state-run **Renfe** (Red Nacional de Ferrocarriles Españoles). Buy your ticket on their website well ahead of travel, particularly for the peak summer season.

There are several routes to Spain from France. Trains from London, Brussels, Amsterdam, Geneva, Zürich and Milan reach Barcelona via Cerbère on the French border with Catalonia. Direct, high-speed luxury TALGO trains, operated by Renfe, go to Barcelona from Paris, Milan, Geneva and Zürich. International trains arrive at Barcelona's Sants mainline station.
Renfe
W renfe.com

Domestic Train Travel

The fastest intercity services are the TALGO and AVE (operated by Renfe), which link Madrid with Barcelona in three hours. Private train operators Ouigo, Iryo and the Renfe subsidiary

vlo also run high-speed trains be-
ween Barcelona and Madrid. AVE
outes link Barcelona with Seville and
Málaga in five and a half hours. The
argo recorrido (long-distance) trains
are cheap but so slow that you usually
reed to travel overnight. *Regionales y
ercanías* (regional and local services)
are frequent and cheap. Overnight
rains are offered by Estrella (a basic
service) to Madrid, and by Trenhotel
(more sophisticated) to A Coruña and
Vigo, in Galicia.

Long-Distance Bus Travel

Often the cheapest way to reach and
ravel around Spain is by coach. Spain
has no national coach company; private
regional companies operate routes
around the country. The largest is
Alsa, with routes and services covering
most of Spain.

Buses from towns and cities in Spain
arrive at Estació del Nord and Sants.
Several companies run day trips or
onger tours around Catalonia. **Turisme
de Catalunya** has details of trips.

Alsa
W alsa.es
Turisme de Catalunya
W catalunyaturisme.cat

Public Transport

Most towns and cities in Catalonia only
offer a bus service, but the larger cities
operate multiple public transport
systems. Barcelona, **Girona**, **Tarragona**
and **Lleida** all have cheap and efficient
bus services (check out the municipal
websites for up-to-date information).
Barcelona also has a well-run metro
system and **FGC** (Ferrocarrils de la
Generalitat de Catalunya) suburban

trains, all run by **TMB** (Transports Metro-
politans de Barcelona). TMB has a useful
interactive website, as well as an app.
Both provide travel information, route
finders, maps and schedules. Metro
maps are also available at stations,
while bus maps are available at the
bigger tourist offices.
FGC
W fgc.cat
Girona
W girona.cat
Lleida
W atmlleida.cat
Tarragona
W emtanemambtu.cat
TMB
W tmb.cat

Tickets

A range of tickets and money-saving
travel cards are available to tourists. The
senzill ticket, for a single journey, can
be used on metro, bus and FGC while
the T-Casual is the most useful for
tourists, allowing ten trips within zone
1 on any metro, bus and FGC (switching
from one mode of transport to another
counts as one journey if done within 75
minutes of validating your ticket). T-Dia
and T-Mes tickets are for unlimited
daily and monthly travel respectively.

Visitors can also enjoy unlimited
journeys through the **Hola Barcelona**
travel cards. There are two-, three-, four-
and five-day options (€16.40, €23.80,
€31 and €38.20 if bought online through
TMB) that can be used on the metro,
FGC and bus. Cards also include the
metro supplement for trips to and
from the airport.
Hola Barcelona Travel Card
W holabarcelona.com

GETTING TO AND FROM THE AIRPORT			
Airport	**Transport**	**Journey Time**	**Price**
Barcelona El Prat Josep Tarradellas	Taxi	20 mins	€30-40
(Terminals 1 & 2)	Aerobús	35 mins	€5.90
(Terminals 1 & 2)	metro	45 mins	€5.15
(Terminal 2)	local train	30 mins	€2.40

Metro

There are eight underground metro lines in Barcelona, usually the quickest way to get around. Platform signs distinguish between trains and their direction by displaying the last station on the line (look out for Renfe and FGC signs at metro stations, which indicate connections to these services). Trains run from 5am to midnight Monday to Thursday, to midnight on Sunday and weekday public holidays, from 5am to 2am on Friday and on the day before a public holiday, and all night on Saturdays.

The L9 metro line connects the city with the airport, and stops at terminals 1 and 2. An airport supplement is charged on this route, and you will not be able to use the T-10 or other standard transport passes. Only the Hola Barcelona pass includes the airport supplement.

Bus

Buses are the most common mode of public transport in Catalonia, but timetables can be erratic. Many services do not run after 10pm, but there are some night buses in the cities.

The main city buses are white and red. Bus numbers beginning with H (for horizontal) run from one side of the city to another and those with V (vertical) run top to bottom; D is diagonal. The Nitbus service runs nightly from around 10:30pm to 5am. Bus maps are available from the main tourist office in Plaça de Catalunya and the TMB website and app.

The privately owned **Aerobús** runs between Plaça de Catalunya and El Prat airport. Public transport passes are not valid on the Aerobús.

Aerobús
W aerobusbarcelona.es

Trams

Barcelona has two tram networks, Trambaix (T1, T2, T3) and Trambesòs (T4, T5, T6), which are operated by **TRAM**. Check their website for operating hours and schedules).

TRAM
W tram.cat

Local Trains

Renfe's network of local trains, *rodalies* in Catalan (*cercanías* in Spanish), is useful for longer distances within Barcelona, particularly between the main train stations: Sants and Estació de França. They are also useful for short hops to Sitges or the northern coastal towns. Maps are displayed at stations, or are available on the Renfe website and app. Trains run 5:30am to 11:30pm daily, but hours vary from line to line. FGC trains run services to Tibidabo, Pedralbes and the Collserola neighbourhoods.

Taxis

Barcelona's taxis are yellow and black, displaying a green light when free. All taxis are metered and show an initial charge of around €2.55. Rates increase between 8pm and 8am, and at weekends and on public holidays. There is a flat rate (€39) for taxis to and from the airport or the Moll Adossat pier. Taxis can be hailed in the street or preorderd via apps such as **Free Now** and **Radio Taxi**. **Taxi Amic** has cars adapted for wheelchair users – note these need to be booked a day ahead.

Free Now
W free-now.com
Radio Taxi
W radiotaxi033.com
Taxi Amic
W taxi-amic.cat

Driving

If you drive to Spain in your own car, you must carry the vehicle's registration document, a valid insurance certificate, a passport or a national identity card and driving licence at all times. You must also display a sticker on the back of the car showing its country of registration.

Driving to Barcelona

Many people drive to Catalonia via France. The most direct routes across the Pyrenees are the motorways through Hendaye in the west and La Jonquera in the east. Port Bou is on a coastal route, while other routes snake ver the top, entering Catalonia via the al d'Aran, Andorra and Puigcerdà in the erdanya. From the UK, car ferries run rom Plymouth to Santander and from ortsmouth to Santander and Bilbao.

Spain has two types of motorway: *utopistas* (toll roads) and *autovías* (toll-ree). If the road prefix is AP there may e a toll but if the prefix is P, it is toll-free.

Carreteras nacionales, Spain's main oads, have black-and-white signs and re designated by the letter N (Nacional) lus a number. *Carreteras comarcales*, econdary roads, have a number receded by the letter C.

Driving in Barcelona

he narrow roads and one-way ystems make driving in the city tricky nd parking can be difficult. The city as a pay-and-display system from am to 2pm and 4pm to 8pm Monday o Friday and all day Saturday. You can ark in blue spaces for about €2.50–.75 per hour. Tickets are valid for two ours but can be renewed. Green paces are reserved for residents permits must be displayed) except nder certain conditions. At under-round car parks, *lliure* means there is pace, *complet* means full. Most are ttended, but in automatic ones, you ay before returning to your car. Do not ark where the pavement edge is yellow r where there is a private exit (*gual*). lue and red signs saying "1–15" or "16–0" mean that you cannot park in the iven areas on those dates of the month.

Car Rental

o rent a car in Barcelona you must ave a valid credit card. Some rental ompanies charge an extra fee to rivers under the age of 25. Major inter-ational car rental agencies have outlets t **Josep Tarradellas Barcelona-El Prat** irport, as well as elsewhere in the city.

Rules of the Road

lost traffic regulations and warnings motorists are represented on signs y easily recognized symbols. To turn left at a busy junction or across oncoming traffic, you may have to turn right first and cross a main road, often by way of traffic lights, a bridge or underpass. If you are accidentally going in the wrong direction on a motorway or a main road with a solid white line, turn round at a sign for a *cambio de sentido*. At crossings, give way to the right unless a sign indicates otherwise.

Cycling

Barcelona has a growing network of cycle lanes that provide access to all the major sights of the city. There are a number of cycle-hire shops, including **Budget Bikes** and **Un Cotxe Menys**. Keep to cycle paths in the city centre, as cycling on roads can be unsafe.

Though **Bicing**, the municipal government-run service, is currently open to residents only, there are several commercial operators who offer rentals to visitors from around €10 for two hours to €60 for a week.

Many bike rental places also conduct cycling tours of the city. **Bike Tours Barcelona** has several themed tours, including a Modernista cycling tour and a beach tour, while **Steel Donkey** focuses on the quirky side of Barcelona.

Bicing
Ⓦ bicing.barcelona

Bike Tours Barcelona
Ⓦ biketoursbarcelona.com

Budget Bikes
Ⓦ budgetbikes.eu

Steel Donkey
Ⓦ steeldonkeybiketours.com

Un Cotxe Menys
Ⓦ biketoursbarcelona.com

Walking

Most areas are best seen on foot, especially the old town, seafront and Gràcia, where a leisurely stroll is the best way to soak up architectural and cultural riches. Try one of the themed walking tours offered by the Barcelona Turisme office. Its website offers an overview of available tours, plus a discount if you buy them online.

PRACTICAL INFORMATION

A little local know-how goes a long way in Barcelona. On these pages you can find all the essential advice and information you will need to make the most of your trip to this city.

AT A GLANCE

CURRENCY
Euro (EUR)

AVERAGE DAILY SPEND

SAVE
€80

SPEND
€150

SPLURGE
€200+

BOTTLED WATER
€0.80

COFFEE
€1

BEER
€2.50

DINNER FOR TWO
€40

ESSENTIAL PHRASES

Hello	Hola/Hola
Goodbye	Adiós/Adéu
Please	Por favor/Si us plau
Thank you	Gracias/Gràcies
Do you speak English?	¿Hablas inglés?/Parles anglès?
I don't understand...	No comprendo/No ho entenc

ELECTRICITY SUPPLY
Power sockets are type F, fitting a two-prong, round-pin plug. Standard voltage is 230 volts.

Passports and Visas

For entry requirements, including visas, consult your nearest Spanish embassy or check the **Ministerio de Asuntos Exteriores** website.

Citizens of the UK, US, Canada, Australia and New Zealand do not need a visa for stays of up to three months, but must apply in advance for the European Travel Information and Authorization System **(ETIAS)**. Visitors from other countries may also require an ETIAS, so check before travelling. EU nationals do not need a visa or an ETIAS.

ETIAS
W etiasvisa.com
Exteriores
W exteriores.gob.es

Government Advice

Now more than ever, it is important to consult both your and the Spanish government's advice before travelling. The **UK Foreign, Commonwealth & Development Office (FCDO)**, the **US Department of State**, the **Australian Department of Foreign Affairs and Trade** and the Exteriores website offer the latest information on security, health and local regulations.

Australian Department of Foreign Affairs and Trade
W smartraveller.gov.au
UK Foreign, Commonwealth & Development Office (FCDO)
W gov.uk/foreigntravel-advice
US Department of State
W travel.state.gov

Customs Information

You can find information on the laws relating to goods and currency taken in or out of Spain on the **Turespaña** (Spain's national tourist board) website.
Turespaña
W spain.info

Insurance

We recommend that you take out a comprehensive insurance policy

overing theft, loss of belongings,
medical care, cancellations and delays,
and read the small print carefully.

EU citizens are eligible for free
emergency medical care in Spain
provided they have a valid European
Health Insurance Card (EHIC) or UK
Global Health Insurance Card **(GHIC)**.

GHIC
◫ ghic.org.uk

Vaccinations
No vaccinations are necessary.

Money
Most urban establishments accept
major credit, debit and prepaid currency
cards. Contactless payments are
common in Barcelona, but it's a good
idea to carry cash for smaller items.
ATMs are widely available, although
many charge for cash withdrawals.
Tipping is not expected for hotel house-
keeping, but porters will expect €1–2 per
bag. Rounding up the fare to the nearest
euro is expected by taxi drivers and it
is usual to tip waiters 5–10 per cent.

Travellers with Specific Requirements
Spain's **COCEMFE** (Confederación
Española de Personas con Discapacidad
Física y Orgánica) provides useful infor-
mation, while companies, such as
Tourism For All and **Accessible Spain**,
offer specialist tours for those with
reduced mobility, sight and hearing.

Spain's public transport system
generally caters for all passengers,
with wheelchairs, adapted toilets,
and reserved car parking available
at airports and stations. Metro maps
in Braille are available from **ONCE**
(Organización Nacional de Ciegos).

Accessible Spain
◫ accessiblespaintravel.com
COCEMFE
◫ cocemfe.es
ONCE
◫ once.es
Tourism For All
◫ tourismforall.org.uk

Language
The two official languages of Catalonia
are *castellano* (Castilian Spanish) and
Catalan. Almost every Catalan can
speak Castilian Spanish, but most
consider Catalan their first language.
As a visitor, it is perfectly acceptable
to speak Castilian wherever you are.
English is widely spoken in the cities
and other tourist spots, but not always
in rural areas.

Opening Hours
Many shops and some museums and
public buildings may close for the siesta,
roughly between 1pm and 5pm. Larger
shops and department stores don't
close at lunchtime and are usually
open until 9 or 10pm.

Many museums, public buildings and
monuments are closed on Monday.
Opening hours for museums and
galleries vary and may change with
the season. It is best to check their
websites before you visit.

On Sundays, churches and cathedrals will generally not permit visitors
during Mass and some public transport
runs less frequently.

Most museums, public buildings
and many shops close early or for
the day on public holidays: New
Year's Day, Epiphany (6 Jan), Good
Friday, Easter Monday, Feast of Sant
Jordi (23 Apr), Labour Day (1 May), Whit
Monday, Feast of Sant Joan (24 Jun),
Ascension Day (15 Aug), Catalan
National Day (11 Sep), Hispanic
Day (12 Oct), All Saints' Day (1 Nov),
Spanish Constitution Day (6 Dec), Feast
of the Immaculate Conception (8 Dec),
Christmas Day (25 Dec), and the Feast
of St Stephen (26 Dec).

Situations can change quickly and
unexpectedly. Always check before
visiting attractions and hospitality
venues for up-to-date opening hours
and booking requirements.

Personal Security

Barcelona is generally a safe city, although petty crimes such as pick-pocketing and bag-snatching remain problematic. Consider leaving your valuables, including passport, in a hotel safety deposit box when out and about. Take particular care at markets, tourist sights and stations, and wear bags and cameras across your body, not on your shoulder. Be especially careful of pickpockets when getting on or off a crowded train or metro.

To report a crime, go to the nearest *comissaria*. Contact is usually with the **Mossos d'Esquadra** (Catalonian police force). Contact your embassy if you have your passport stolen, or in the event of a serious crime or accident.

Barcelona is a diverse, multicultural city and, as a rule, Catalans are very accepting of all people, regardless of their race, gender or sexuality. Homo-sexuality was legalized in 1979 and Spain was the third country to legalize same-sex marriage, in 2005. In 2007, Spain recognized the right to legally change your gender. Barcelona has a flourishing LGBTQ+ scene centred on "Gaixample" (part of L'Eixample). If you do feel unsafe, the **Safe Space Alliance** pinpoints your nearest place of refuge.

Mossos d'Esquadra
📞 112
Safe Space Alliance
🌐 safespacealliance.com

Health

Spain has a world-class healthcare system. Emergency medical care in Spain is free for all EU and UK citizens. If you have an EHIC or GHIC *(p141)*, be sure to present this as soon as possible. You may have to pay after treatment and reclaim the money later. For other visitors, payment of medical expenses is the patient's responsibility. It is there-fore important to arrange comprehen-sive medical insurance before travelling.

For medicinal supplies and minor ailments, go to a *farmàcia* (pharmacy), identified by a red or green cross. When closed, they will post a sign with the add-ress of the nearest all-night pharmacy.

Smoking, Alcohol and Drugs

Smoking is banned in enclosed public spaces and on beaches and is a fineable offence, although you can still smoke on the terraces of bars and restaurants

Spain has a relaxed attitude towards alcohol consumption, but it is frowned upon to be openly drunk.

Most recreational drugs are illegal, and possession of even a very small quantity can lead to an extremely hefty fine. Amounts that suggest an intent to supply drugs to other people can lead to custodial sentences. Cannabis clubs can supply the drug to members, but it's illegal to smoke it in public spaces.

ID

By law you must carry identification with you at all times in Spain. A photocopy of your passport should suffice. If stopped by the police, you may be asked to report to a police station with the original.

Responsible Tourism

The climate crisis is having a big impact on Barcelona, with increasingly frequent droughts and heatwaves. Fountains, whether for drinking water or for decoration, may be turned off and shows at the Font Màgica may be suspended in times of drought. Do your bit by taking quick showers and reusing towels if staying in a hotel. Catalonia is also at risk of wildfires so be careful when disposing of cigarette butts and glass bottles; starting a fire, even if accidental, is a criminal offence.

Local Customs

Regional pride is strong throughout Spain. Be wary of referring to Catalans as "Spanish", as this may cause offence.

Visiting Churches and Cathedrals

Generally, entrance to churches is free; though a fee may apply to enter special areas, like cloisters. Out of respect, ensure that you are dressed modestly when visiting religious buildings, with knees and shoulders covered.

Mobile Phones and Wi-Fi

Free Wi-Fi is reasonably common, particularly in libraries, large public spaces, restaurants and bars. Some places, such as airports and hotels, may charge for using their Wi-Fi. The city council provides free Wi-Fi throughout much of the city centre and in metro stations and buses, but bandwidth is limited. Use the **WiFi Map** website and app to find Wi-Fi hotspots near you.

Visitors on EU tariffs can use the 4G or 5G mobile network without being affected by roaming charges.

WiFi Map
w wifimap.io

Postal Services

Correos is Spain's postal service. Stamps can be purchased from a post office, a *papelería* (stationery shop) or an *estanco* (tobacconist). Parcels must be weighed and stamped at Correos offices.

Letters sent from a post office usually arrive more quickly than if posted in a *buzón* (postbox). In cities, postboxes are yellow pillar boxes; elsewhere they are wall-mounted postboxes.

Correos
w correos.es

Taxes and Refunds

IVA (VAT) is normally 21 per cent, but with lower rates for certain goods and services, such as hotels and restaurants. Under certain conditions, non-EU citizens can claim a rebate of these taxes. Retailers can give you a form to fill out, which you can then present to a customs officer with your receipts as you leave. Some shops offer DIVA (digital stamping technology), which can be validated at self-service machines in the airport.

Discount Cards

Barcelona offers the **Barcelona Card**, a visitor's pass that includes entry to the city's top museums and unlimited free travel on public transport, plus discounts at participating restaurants, shops and on tours. It can also help you skip queues and is valid for three (€48), four (€58) or five (€63) consecutive days.

Barcelona Card
w barcelonacard.org

PLACES TO STAY

From dazzling designer hotels to cozy family-run guesthouses, Barcelona has a hotel for every type of traveller in each of the city's unique neighbourhoods.

Prices are usually highest at Easter, Christmas and in summer, but the shoulder seasons around April–May and September–October are ideal thanks to fewer visitors and mild temperatures. A tourist tax is payable (for guests aged 17+, maximum for 7 days), with a sliding scale depending on the type of accommodation.

PRICE CATEGORIES

For a standard, double room per night (with breakfast if included), taxes and extra charges.

€ under €250
€€ $250–€450
€€€ over €450

Barri Gòtic and La Riber

Soho House

🅿 L6 🏠 Pl del Duc de Medinaceli 4 🌐 soho-house.com/houses/soho-house-barcelona · €€€

Celebrity boltholes don't come more fabulous than this 18th-century town-house, with its glorious vaulted ceilings and style that combines traditional Catalan tiles and warm Mediterranean colours. Luxury facilities include a cowshed spa and gym, an in-house cinema with lavish velvet armchairs and a rooftop bar for (discreet) star-spotting.

Kimpton Vividora

🅿 M2 🏠 Carrer del Duc 15 🌐 himptonvividorahotel.com · €€€

Vividora means someone who lives life to the fullest, and this fashionable hotel will help you do just that. Want to hire a skateboard? No problem. In the mood for a rooftop concert? You're in luck. Bringing a pet? All animals are welcome – so long as they fit in the lift.

Hotel Barcelona Catedral

🅿 M3 🏠 Carrer dels Capellans 4 🌐 barcelona-catedral.com · €€

It doesn't get much more central than this. Slap bang in the heart of the Gothic Quarter, this welcoming hotel has great-value rooms that are more spacious than most in the cramped old city, and all are sound-proofed. Great for if you need to block out Barcelona's signature buzz.

Chic&Basic Habana Hoose

🅿 N4 🏠 C/de l'Argenteria, 37 🌐 hicandbasic.com/es/hotel-habana-hoose-barcelona · €€

Cuba and Scotland don't make for an obvious combination but it works a treat at this delightfully eccentric hotel set in an 18th-century mansion. The Cuban touches may be difficult to discern, but you can't miss the many flashes of tartan amid the sage green-panelling of the rooms (even the lift is lined with tartan).

H10 Cubik

🅿 N2 🏠 Via Laietana 69 🌐 h10hotels.com · €€

H10 are experts in helping guests unwind after a long day, which starts with a complimentary glass of *cava* on arrival. Once you've finished that first drink head up to the rooftop bar for the hotel's signature cocktail and tapas as the sun disappears behind the surrounding buildings.

Ciutat de Barcelona

🅿 P4 🏠 C/Princesa 33-35 🌐 ciutatbarcelona.com · €

If you want to be in the thick of the action choose the Ciutat de Barcelona. Step just beyond its threshold and you'll be among the independent boutiques and trendy cafés and bars of the Born neighbourhood. Oh, and did we mention the Picasso Museum is round the corner?

Motel One Barcelona Ciutadella

🅿 Q3 🏠 Pg. de Pujades 11-13 📞 936 26 19 00 · €

Motel One may look unremarkable from the

outside, but inside it's an artistic wonderland. Striking murals by local illustrator Lara Costafreda depict jungle scenes and famous landmarks to give each room a unique feel, while the lobby features carved wood and textile patterns, all complimented by abundant plants.

El Raval

Casa Camper

📍 L2 🏠 C/Elisabets 11
🌐 casacamper.com · €€€

Who knew shoes also did hotels? Casa Camper, owned by the Camper shoe company, was among the first hotels in the city to prioritize sustainability. Today, you'll find a 24-hour buffet and honesty bar instead of wasteful mini bars in the rooms, large, refillable toiletries in the bathrooms and an abundance of vegetation in the chill-out zone.

Hotel Bagués

📍 M2 🏠 La Rambla 105
🌐 hotelbagues.com · €€€

This plush retreat on La Rambla is everything you'd want from a luxury stay. Personalized service recalls a bygone era and rooms are exquisitely appointed in dark wood and gold leaf. The hotel's building even has a luxurious history: it was previously the headquarters of Bagués-Masriera jewellers and still displays some of the more exquisite pieces around the hotel.

Antiga Casa Buenvista

📍 D3 🏠 Ronda de Sant Antoni 84 🌐 hotelcasa-buenavista.com · €€

Sustainability is at the heart of this boutique hotel run by the Molleví family. You won't find single-use plastics or paper, solar panels power the low-energy lighting, and the hotel sources local ingredients for its minibars and excellent restaurant. And when you want to explore the city there are electric scooters for hire.

Hotel España

📍 K4 🏠 C/Sant Pau 9-11,
🌐 hotelespanya.com · €€

Lovers of the Modernista aesthetic should make a beeline for this mosaic-filled hotel. The interior includes enchanting murals designed by Domènech i Montaner, including the "hall of Mermaids", perhaps the most beautiful dining setting in the city.

Hotel Market

📍 D4 🏠 C/Comte Borrell 68
🌐 hotelmarketbarcelona.com · €

Hotel Market is proof that budget stays can also be glamorous. An elegant chandelier hangs over the lobby, evoking the grandeur of the original 19th-century building, while the funky rooms combine elegant dark wood and bright red accents. Put on your glad rags and take a seat at the little cocktail bar.

Ciutat Vella

📍 L1 🏠 C/Tallers 66
🌐 hotelciutatvella.com · €

A friendly budget hotel is always a safe bet and the Ciutat Vella is just that. Rooms may lack high-end features but still feature comfy beds and flat-screen TVs. Some even include a small balcony or private terrace. Ascend to the small roof terrace and you'll find a jacuzzi where you can kickback and soak up the sun.

Montjuïc

Hotel Miramar

📍 C5 🏠 Plaça de Carlos Ibáñez 3 🌐 hotelmiramar-barcelona.com · €€€

You might not be royalty, but that doesn't mean you can't stay in this converted 1920s palace. Settle in and enjoy the seemingly endless list of luxuries on offer, including a relaxing spa, fine dining restaurant and outdoor pool set in curated gardens.

Hotel Brummell

📍 C5 🏠 Carrer Nou de la Rambla 174 🌐 hotel-brummell.com · €€

Tucked away in the lively Poble Sec neighbourhood, this independent boutique hotel packs a lot into a small space. A social media-worthy courtyard garden for morning coffee, a compact rooftop pool and an honesty bar. Try a yoga class or work up a sweat at a boxing lesson, both are free.

The Seafront

W Barcelona

🅖 E6 🏠 Plaça Rosa Del Vents 1 🅦 marriott.com/en-us/hotels/bcnwh-w-barcelona · €€€

You really can't miss this iconic hotel, located in a gleaming sail-shaped building by the beach. Rooms, particularly those on the upper floors, give you the sense of sleeping atop the mast, and the facilities tick every five-star box you can think of, particularly the famous bar high up in the clouds on the 27th floor.

Arts

🅖 G6 🏠 Carrer de la Marina 19–21 🅦 hotelartsbarcelona.com · €€€

The Arts has been among the city's best hotels since this glittering skyscraper was built for the 1992 Olympics. The facilities are world-class, rooms offer panoramic views (some even come with a private butler) and the glamorous outdoor pool is overlooked by a Frank Gehry fish sculpture.

Hotel Oasis

🅖 P5 🏠 Pla del Palau 17 · €€

Need an excellently located base from which to explore the delightful city centre attractions? Hotel Oasis is that place. Staying here means you're minutes from the main sites of the old town. Perhaps you'll want to hit the hotspots of La Rambla or head the other way to the best beaches in Barceloneta.

Eixample

El Palace

🅖 F3 🏠 Gran Via de les Corts Catalanes 668 🅦 hotelpalacebarcelona.com · €€€

The undisputed grande dame of Barcelona hotels, this stately mansion (formerly the Ritz) is a lavish swirl of red velvet, glittering chandeliers and top-hatted doormen, and that's before you even reach the rooms. Choose your room wisely: suites are named after celebrity guests from Josephine Baker to Ronnie Wood.

Mandarin Hotel

🅖 E3 🏠 Passeig de Gràcia 38–40 🅦 mandarin-oriental.com/en/barcelona · €€€

Thanks to legendary design star Patricia Urquiola, the Mandarin has become a style icon in Barcelona – even the entrance is a gold catwalk. Once you've hit the runway, head to the hotel's two-Michelin-star restaurant Moments, where chef Raúl Balam will whisk you away with a menu that follows La Vuelta cycling race across Spain.

Margot House

🅖 E2 🏠 Passeig de Gràcia 46 🅦 margothouse.es · €€

Named after a character in the Wes Anderson film *The Royal Tenenbaums*, this delightful nine-room boutique hotel channels Anderson's quirky aesthetic through a unique interior that pairs Nordic design with a mish-mash of prints and sculptures. Perhaps it's appropriate that it stands opposite Gaudí's equally quirky Casa Batlló.

Granados 83

🅖 E2 🏠 C/Enric Granados 83 🅦 hotelgranados83.com · €€

What to do with a former hospital? Well, one option is to turn it into an eclectic art deco hotel such as this. Where once there were hard beds in cold wards, now the beds are soft and inviting while the former wards are welcoming rooms filled with exposed brick, dark African wood and Hindu and Buddhist art.

Casa Bonay

🅖 F3 🏠 Gran Via de les Corts Catalanes 700 🅦 casabonay.com · €€

Every nook and cranny of this hipster hangout oozes quirky charm, making it a magnet for the trendy and cool. Once you've got shots of the room for your social media, head to the louche, velvety café and bar on the ground floor or ascend to the rooftop eyrie of wicker armchairs and floral sofas.

Hotel Jazz

🅖 L1 🏠 C/Pelai 3 🅦 hotel-jazz.com · €€

What makes the modest Hotel Jazz a winner? First, there's the spectacular location, just off the Plaça Catalunya. Second, it's filled with minimalist but comfortable rooms. And third, the friendly staff make every stay memorable. Put it all together and this is one of the best places to stay in the city.

Praktik Garden

F3 **C/Diputació 325** **hotelprahtihgarden. com · €**

Praktik Garden really lives up to the garden part. Plant motifs are found everywhere from the botanic prints that decorate the hotel to the actual plants that adorn the lovely courtyard garden, rooftop terrace and lobby, the latter alongside wacky floor-to-ceiling circus posters.

Hostal Oliva

E3 **Passeig de Gràcia 32** **hostaloliva.com · €**

Those wanting some old-fashioned charm will love Hostal Olivia. Everything exudes history, from the beautiful belle époque building to the antique cast-iron lift. The rooms are compact, but given the affordable price and great location, you'll find this place hard to resist.

Gràcia, Tibidabo and Zona Alta

Hotel Veritas

E1 **Passeig de Gràcia 132** **hotelcasafuster. com · €€€**

This landmark Modernista mansion was the most expensive in the city when it was built in 1904. While it no longer retains that dubious honour, it does still have something few others can match: an architect responsible for

multiple UNESCO World Heritage Sites in Domènech i Montaner.

La Casa del Sol

F1 **Plaça del Sol 23** **sonder.com/destin-ations/barcelona/bcn-sol23-11/c31099 · €€**

The Gràcia neighbourhood is famous for its squares, and this hotel overlooks the best: the Plaça del Sol, packed with tapas bars and cafés. Hop from bar to bar, sampling all the local dishes, and when you need a break, retreat to the rooftop terrace to watch the action from above.

Casa Gràcia

E1 **Passeig de Gràcia 116** **casagraciabcn. com · €**

Rarely does a hotel build a true community, but this place is all about getting to know your fellow guests. Make friends with your roommates while you sink into bean bags in the communal zen room or hire bikes and take a group pedal across town.

Beyond Barcelona

Hotel Aiguaclara

Carrer Sant Miquel 2, Begur **hotelaigua-clarabegur.com · €€€**

Set in a handsome 19th-century villa in fashionable Begur, and with only ten elegantly furnished rooms, Hotel Aiguaclara can feel like your own private retreat. So take time for yourself on the terrace or enjoy

delicious Catalan cuisine in the restaurant. But if you do fancy an outing, the glorious Costa Brava is only ten minutes away.

Casa Vilella

Passeig Marítim 21, Sitges **hotelcasavilella. com · €€€**

With an unbeatable location right on the seafront in Sitges, this hotel makes lazy beach days easy. And if that short walk to the beach is just a bit too far? The on-site garden and pool, excellent restaurant and well-appointed spa have you covered.

Nord 1901

C/Nord 7-9, Girona **nord1901.com · €€**

You won't find a friendlier stay than at Nord. It's been run by the same family since it was established in 1901 and they've crafted an atmosphere dedicated to making you feel at home. No request is too much – the staff have the attentive care that is only given when staying with family.

Hostal 977

Carrer dels Cavallers 4, Tarragona **hostal 977.com · €**

Like your city stays a little rustic? Then you'll love Hostal 977. This pretty, family-run guesthouse will make you feel like you're in the countryside with its exposed stone walls and wood beams. And the best bit? The sights of Tarragona's old town are on the doorstep.

INDEX

CATALAN PHRASE BOOK

In an Emergency

Help!	Auxili!	ow-**gzee**-lee
Stop!	Pareu!	**pah**-reh-oo
Call a doctor!	Telefoneu un metge!	teh-leh-fon-**eh**-oo oon **meh**-djuh
Call an ambulance!	Telefoneu una ambulància!	teh-leh-fon-**eh**-oo oo-nah ahm-boo-**lahn**-see-ah
Call the police!	Telefoneu la policía	teh-leh-fon-**eh**-oo lah poh-lee-**see**-ah
Call the fire brigade!	Telefoneu els bombers!	teh-leh-fon-eh-oo uhlz boom-**behs**
Where is the nearest telephone?	On és el telèfon més proper?	**on**-ehs uhl **teh**-leh **fon mehs** proo-**peh**
Where is the nearest hospital?	On és l'hospital més proper?	**on**-ehs looss-pee-**tahl mehs** proo-**peh**

Communication Essentials

Yes	Sí	see
No	No	noh
Please	Si us plau	sees **plah**-oo
Thank you	Gràcies	**grah**-see-uhs
Excuse me	Perdoni	puhr-**thoh**-nee
Hello	Hola	**oh**-lah
Goodbye	Adéu	ah-they-**oo**
Good night	Bona nit	bo-nah neet
Morning	El matí	uhl muh-**tee**
Afternoon	La tarda	lah **tahr**-thuh
Evening	El vespre	uhl **vehs**-pruh
Yesterday	Ahir	ah-**ee**
Today	Avui	uh-voo-ee
Tomorrow	Demà	duh-**mah**
Here	Aquí	uh-**kee**
There	Allà	uh-**lyah**
What?	Què?	keh
When?	Quan?	kwahn
Why?	Per què?	puhr keh
Where?	On?	ohn

Useful Phrases

How are you?	Com està?	kom uhs-**tah**
Very well, thank you.	Molt bé, gràcies.	mol beh **grah**-see-uhs
Pleased to meet you.	Molt de gust.	mol duh **goost**
See you soon.	Fins aviat.	feenz uhv-**yat**
Where is/are..?	On és/són?	ohn ehs/sohn
How far is it to?	Quants metres/ kilòmetres hi ha d'aquí a...?	kwahnz meh-truhs/kee-**loh**-muh-truhs yah dah-**kee** uh

Which way to...?	Per on es va a...?	puhr **on** uhs **bah** ah
Do you speak English?	Parla anglès?	**par**-luh an-**glehs**
I don't understand	No l'entenc.	noh luhn-**teng**
Could you speak more slowly, please?	Pot parlar més a poc a poc, si us plau?	pot par-**lah mehs** pok uh pok sees **plah**-oo
I'm sorry.	Ho sento.	oo **sehn**-too

Useful Words

big	gran	gran
small	petit	puh-**teet**
hot	calent	kah-**len**
cold	fred	fred
good	bo	boh
bad	dolent	doo-**len**
enough	bastant	bahs-**tan**
well	bé	beh
open	obert	oo-**behr**
closed	tancat	tan-**kat**
left	esquerra	uhs-**kehr**-ruh
right	dreta	**dreh**-tuh
straight on	recte	**rehk**-tuh
near	a prop	uh **prop**
far	lluny	**lyoon**yuh
up/over	a dalt	uh **dahl**
down/under	a baix	uh **bah**-eeshh
early	aviat	uhv-**yat**
late	tard	**tahrt**
entrance	entrada	uhn-**trah**-thuh
exit	sortida	**soor**-tee-thuh
toilet	lavabos/ serveis	luh-**vah**-boos sehr-**beh**-ees
more	més	mess
less	menys	**men**yees

Shopping

How much does this cost?	Quant costa això?	kwahn kost ehs-**shoh**
I would like...	M'agradaria...	muh-grah-**thuh**-ree-ah
Do you have?	Tenen?	**tehn**-un
I'm just looking, thank you	Només estic mirant, gràcies.	noo-mess ehs-**teek** mee-**rahn grah**-see-uhs
Do you take credit cards?	Accepten targes de crèdit?	ak-**sehp**-tuhn tahr-**zhuhs** duh **kreh**-deet
What time do you open?	A quina hora obren?	ah **keen**-uh oh-ruh oh-**bruhn**

What time do you close?	**A quina hora tanquen?**	*ah keen-uh oh -ruh tan-kuhn*
This one.	**Aquest**	*ah-ket*
That one.	**Aquell**	*ah-kehl*
That's fine.	**Està bé.**	*uhs-tah beh*
expensive	**car**	*kahr*
cheap	**bé de preu/ barat**	*beh thuh preh-oo/bah-rat*
size (clothes)	**talla/mida**	*tah-lyah/ mee-thuh*
size (shoes)	**número**	*noo-mehr-oo*
white	**blanc**	*blang*
black	**negre**	*neh-gruh*
red	**vermell**	*vuhr-mel*
yellow	**groc**	*grok*
green	**verd**	*behrt*
blue	**blau**	*blah-oo*
antique store	**antiquari/ botiga d'antiguitats**	*an-tee-kwah-ree/ boo-tee-gah/ dan-tee-ghee-tats*
bakery	**el forn**	*uhl forn*
bank	**el banc**	*uhl bang*
book store	**la llibreria**	*lah lyee-bruh-ree-ah*
butcher's	**la carnisseria**	*lah kahr-nee-suh-ree-ah*
pastry shop	**la pastisseria**	*lah pahs-tee-suh-ree-uh*
chemist's	**la farmàcia**	*lah fuhr-mah-see-ah*
fishmonger's	**la peixateria**	*lah peh-shuh-tuh-ree-uh*
greengrocer's	**la fruiteria**	*lah froo-ee-tuh-ree-uh*
grocer's	**la botiga de queviures**	*lah boo-tee-guh duh keh-vee-oo-ruhs*
hairdresser's	**la perruqueria**	*lah peh-roo-kuh-ree-uh*
market	**el mercat**	*uhl muhr-kat*
newsagent's	**el quiosc de premsa**	*uhl kee-ohsk duh prem-suh*
post office	**l'oficina de correus**	*loo-fee-see-nuh duh koo-reh-oos*
shoe store	**la sabateria**	*lah sah-bah-tuh-ree-uh*
supermarket	**el supermercat**	*uhl soo-puhr-muhr-kat*
travel agency	**l'agència de viatges**	*la-jen-see-uh duh vee-ad-juhs*

Sightseeing

art gallery	**la galeria d' art**	*lah gah-luh ree-yuh dart*
cathedral	**la catedral**	*lah kuh-tuh-thrahl*
church	**l'església**	*luhz-gleh-zee-uh*
garden	**el jardí**	*uhl zhahr-dee*
library	**la biblioteca**	*lah bee-blee-oo-teh-kuh*

museum	**el museu**	*uhl moo-seh-oo*
tourist information office	**l'oficina de turisme**	*loo-fee-see-nuh thuh too-reez -muh*
town hall	**l'ajuntament**	*luh-djoon-tuh-men*
closed for holiday	**tancat per vacances**	*tan-kat puhr bah-kan-suhs*
bus station	**l'estació d'autobusos**	*luhs-tah-see-oh dow-toh-boo-zoos*
railway station	**l'estació de tren**	*luhs-tah-see-oh thuh tren*

Staying in a Hotel

Do you have a vacant room?	**¿Tenen una habitació lliure?**	*teh-nuhn oo-nuh ah-bee-tuh-see-oh lyuh-ruh*
double room with double bed	**habitació doble amb llit de matrimoni**	*ah-bee-tuh-see-oh doh-bluh am lyeet duh mah-tree-moh-nee*
twin room	**habitació amb dos llits/ amb llits individuals**	*ah-bee-tuh-see-oh am dohs lyeets/am lyeets in-thee-vee thoo-ahls*
single room	**habitació individual**	*ah-bee-tuh-see-oh een-dee-vee-thoo-ahl*
room with	**habitació**	*ah-bee-tuh-see-oh*
a bath	**amb bany**	*am bahnyuh*
shower	**dutxa**	*doo-chuh*
porter	**el grum**	*uhl groom*
key	**la clau**	*lah klah-oo*
I have a reservation	**Tinc una habitació reservada**	*ting oo-nuh ah-bee-tuh-see -oh reh-sehr-vah -thah*

Eating Out

Have you got a table for…	**Tenen taula per…?**	*teh-nuhn tow-luh puhr*
I would like to reserve a table.	**Voldria reservar una taula.**	*vool-dree-uh reh-sehr-vahr oo-nuh tow-luh*
The bill please	**El compte, si us plau.**	*uhl kohm-tuh sees plah-oo*
I am a vegetarian	**Sóc vegetarià/ vegetariana**	*sok buh-zhuh-tuh-ree-ah/buh-zhuh -tuh-ree-ah-nah*
waitress	**cambrera**	*kam-breh-ruh*
waiter	**cambrer**	*kam-breh*
menu	**la carta**	*lah kahr-tuh*

fixed-price menu	menú del migdia	muh-**noo** thuhl meech-**dee**-uh
wine list	la carta de vins	ah **kahr**-tuh thuh **veens**
glass of water	un got d'aigua	oon **got** dah-ee-gwah
glass of wine	una copa de vi	**oo**-nuh **ko**-pah thuh **vee**
bottle	una ampolla	**oo**-nuh am-**pol**-yuh
knife	un ganivet	oon gun-ee-**veht**
fork	una forquilla	**oo**-nuh foor-**keel**-yuh
spoon	una cullera	**oo**-nuh kool-**yeh**-ruh
breakfast	l'esmorzar	les-moor-**sah**
lunch	el dinar	uhl dee-**nah**
dinner	el sopar	uhl soo-**pah**
main course	el primer plat	uhl pree-**meh plat**
starters	els entrants	uhlz ehn-**tranz**
dish of the day	el plat del dia	uhl **plat** duhl **dee**-uh
coffee	el cafè	uhl kah-**feh**
rare	poc fet	**pok fet**
medium	al punt	ahl **poon**
well done	molt fet	mol **fet**

Menu Decoder

l'aigua mineral	**lah**-ee-gwuh mee-nuh-**rahl**	mineral water
sense gas/ amb gas	sen-zuh gas/ am gas	still sparkling
al forn	ahl **forn**	baked
l'all	**lahl**yuh	garlic
l'arròs	lahr-**roz**	rice
les botifarres	lahs **boo**-tee-fah-rahs	sausages
la carn	lah **karn**	meat
la ceba	lah **seh**-buh	onion
la cervesa	lah-sehr-**ve**-sah	beer
l'embotit	lum-boo-**teet**	cold meat
el filet	uhl **fee**-let	sirloin
el formatge	uhl for-**mah**-djuh	cheese
fregit	freh-**zheet**	fried
la fruita	lah froo-**ee**-tah	fruit
els fruits secs	uhlz froo-**eets seks**	nuts
les gambes	lahs **gam**-bus	prawns
el gelat	uhl djuh-**lat**	ice cream
la llagosta	lah lyah-**gos**-tah	lobster
la llet	lah **lyet**	milk
la llimona	lah lyee-**moh**-nah	lemon
la llimonada	lah lyee-moh-**nah**-tuh	lemonade
la mantega	lah mahn-**teh**-gah	butter

el marisc	uhl muh-**reesk**	seafood
la menestra	lah muh-**nehs**-truh	vegetable stew
l'oli	**loll**-ee	oil
les olives	luhs oo-**lee**-vuhs	olives
l'ou	**loh**-oo	egg
el pa	uhl **pah**	bread
el pastís	uhl pahs-**tees**	pie/cake
les patates	lahs **pah**-tah-tuhs	potatoes
el pebre	uhl **peh**-bruh	pepper
el peix	uhl **pehsh**	fish
el pernil salat serrà	uhl puhr-**neel** suh-**lat** sehr-**rah**	cured ham
el plàtan	uhl **plah**-tun	banana
el pollastre	uhl poo-**lyah**-struh	chicken
la poma	la **poh**-mah	apple
el porc	uhl **pohr**	pork
les postres	lahs **pohs**-truhs	dessert
rostit	rohs-**teet**	roast
la sal	lah **sahl**	salt
la salsa	lah **sahl**-suh	sauce
les salsitxes	lahs sahl-**see**-chuhs	sausages
sec	**sehk**	dry
la sopa	lah **soh**-puh	soup
el sucre	uhl-**soo**-kruh	sugar
la taronja	lah tuh-**rohn**-djuh	orange
el te	uhl **teh**	tea
les torrades	lahs too-**rah**-thuhs	toast
la vedella	lah veh-**theh**-lyuh	beef
el vi blanc	uhl **bee blang**	white wine
el vi negre	uhl **bee neh**-gruh	red wine
el vi rosat	uhl **bee** roo-**zaht**	rosé wine
el vinagre	uhl bee-**nah**-gruh	vinegar
el xai/el be	uhl **shahee**/ uhl **beh**	lamb
la xocolata	lah shoo-koo-**lah**-tuh	chocolate
el xoriç	uhl shoo-**rees**	red sausage

Numbers

0	zero	**seh**-roo
1	un (masc)	**oon**
	una (fem)	**oon**-uh
2	dos (masc)	**dohs**
	dues (fem)	**doo**-uhs
3	tres	**trehs**
4	quatre	**kwa**-truh
5	cinc	**seeng**
6	sis	**sees**
7	set	**set**
8	vuit	**voo**-eet
9	nou	**noh**-oo
10	deu	**deh**-oo

11	onze	*on*-zuh
12	dotze	*doh*-dzuh
13	tretze	*treh*-dzuh
14	catorze	kah-*tohr*-dzuh
15	quinze	*keen*-zuh
16	setze	*set*-zuh
17	disset	dee-*set*
18	divuit	dee-voo-*eet*
19	dinou	dee-*noh*-oo
20	vint	*been*
21	vint-i-un	*been-tee-oon*
22	vint-i-dos	*been-tee-dohs*
30	trenta	*tren*-tah
31	trenta-un	*tren*-tah *oon*
40	quaranta	kwuh-*ran*-tuh
50	cinquanta	seen-*kwahn*-tah
60	seixanta	seh-ee-*shan*-tah
70	setanta	seh-*tan*-tah
80	vuitanta	voo-ee-*tan*-tah
90	noranta	noh-*ran*-tah
100	cent	*sen*
101	cent un	*sent oon*
102	cent dos	*sen dohs*

200	dos-cents	*dohs-sens*
	dues-centes (fem)	*doo*-uhs *sen*-tuhs
300	tres-cents	*trehs-senz*
400	quatre-cents	*kwah-truh-senz*
500	cinc-cents	*seeng-senz*
600	sis-cents	*sees-senz*
700	set-cents	*set-senz*
800	vuit-cents	*voo-eet-senz*
900	nou-cents	*noh-oo-cenz*
1,000	mil	*meel*
1,001	mil un	*meel oon*

Time

one minute	un minut	*oon mee-noot*
one hour	una hora	*oo-nuh oh-ruh*
half an hour	mitja hora	*mee-juh oh-ruh*
Monday	dilluns	*dee-lyoonz*
Tuesday	dimarts	*dee-marts*
Wednesday	dimecres	*dee-meh-kruhs*
Thursday	dijous	*dee-zhoh-oos*
Friday	divendres	*dee-ven-druhs*
Saturday	dissabte	*dee-sab-tuh*
Sunday	diumenge	*dee-oo-men-juh*

ACKNOWLEDGMENTS

This edition updated by

Contributor Mary-Ann Gallagher

Senior Editors Alison McGill, Dipika Dasgupta

Project Editor Anuroop Sanwaila

Senior Designers Laura O'Brien, Vinita Venugopal

Art Editor Bandana Paul

Editors Charlie Baker, Anjasi N.N.

Assistant Editor Vineet Singh

Proofreader Stephanie Smith

Indexer Kathryn O'Donoghue

Picture Research Manager Taiyaba Khatoon

Senior Picture Researcher Nishwan Rasool

Assistant Picture Research Administrator Manpreet Kaur

Publishing Assistant Simona Velikova

Jacket Designer Laura O'Brien

Jacket Picture Researcher Kate Hockenhull

Senior Cartographic Editor James Macdonald

Cartography Simonetta Giori

Senior DTP Designer Tanveer Zaidi

DTP Designer Rohit Rojal

Pre Production Manager Balwant Singh

Image Retouching-Production Manager Pankaj Sharma

Senior Production Controller Samantha Cross

Managing Editors Shikha Kulkarni, Beverly Smart, Hollie Teague

Managing Art Editor Gemma Doyle

Senior Managing Art Editor Priyanka Thakur

Art Director Maxine Pedliham

Publishing Director Georgina Dee

DK would like to thank the following for their contribution to the previous editions: AnneLise Sorensen, Ryan Chandler, Paula Canal, Kate Berens, Hilary Bird.

The publisher would like to thank the following for their kind permission to reproduce their photographs:

Key: a-above; b-below/bottom; c-center; f-far; l-left; r-right; t-top

Alamy Stock Photo: Rubens Alarcon 34b, Album 9cr, 13cla (7), Sara Aribó / Pximages / Associated Press 13cla, Sergio Azenha 85, Classic Image 9tl, Ian Dagnall 28t, 28b, David Zorrakino / Associated Press 10bl, dleiva 19, Rosmi Duaso 125, eye35 58t, Luke Farmer 32clb, Christophe Faugre 63b, Fine Art Images / Heritage Images 25clb, Peter Forsberg 94, Kevin Foy 13tl, frantic 58tl, Jeffrey Isaac Greenberg 7+ 69, Patrice Hauser / Hemis.fr 114tl, John Henshall 35br, Heritage Image Partnership Ltd 9br, Silvia Isach 60, Jeffrey Isaac Greenberg 5+ 12br, Tim Langlotz / Image Professionals GmbH 64, Javier Larrea 12crb, Lenski / Panther Media GmbH 13cl, Little valleys 112tl, Melvyn Longhurst 58–59b, Iophius 11br, Stefano Politi Markovina 21bl, 24t, 41, 62tr, 70, 86, 103, Ren Mattes / Hemis.fr 89, Hercules Milas 99, Nathaniel Noir 119tr, Matthias Oesterle 74, PePoP 35t, PhotoBliss 8b, Prisma Archivo 9tr, M Ramrez 43br, 88, Juergen Richter / Image Professionals GmbH 31tr, © Successió Miró / ADAGP, Paris and DACS London 2024 37, 106–107b, Marc Soler 123, SOPA Images 43bl, Marek Stepan 112–113b, Topseee 106tl, Lucas Vallecillos 57, Jan Wlodarczyk 5, 14, 15t, 21tl.

AWL Images: Hemis 42, Sabine Lubenow 22t.

Bar Muy Buenas: 96.

Bobby Gin: Pau Esculies 124.

Boo: 122.

Bridgeman Images: © Succession Picasso / DACS, London 2024 39br.

Bus Terraza: 65b.

Dorling Kindersley: Departure Lounge / Museu d'Art Contemporani (MACBA), Barcelona 43cb, Palau de la Musica Catalana, Barcelona 41b.

Dreamstime.com: Igor Abramovych 102, Alexvaneekelen 84, Steve Allen 51bl, 91br, Davide Bonaldo 67br, Boule13 12cra, Marco Brivio 66tl, Castecodesign 82, Chbm89 77, Demerzel21 100, Dudlajzov 81tl, Elovkoff 13clb, Elxeneize 22bl, Marta Fernndez 76, Iakov Filimonov 49, 72, 83bl, Gazzag 56b, Skrypko Ievgen 121bl, Gábor Kovács 127t, Lanaufoto 131, Lunamarina 66–67b, Marcorubino 21crb, 52, Matteocozzi 46tl, Anamaria Mejia 20c, 27br, Lucian Milasan 33br, Juan Moyano 108, William Perry 130, Jure Porenta 120, Sanguer 55bl, 132, Jacek Sopotnicki 93tl, Tanaonte 75, Thecriss 34cra, Tomas1111 46br, 50, Vicnt 101bl, Noppasin Wongchum 92b.

Els Pescadors: 133.

Getty Images: adoc-photos / Corbis 10br, Pol Albarrán 111t, Dan Kitwood 10clb, David Madison 10cla, Mario Marco 13bl, Rolls Press / Popperfoto 11t, Alexander Spatari 63tr, 79.

Getty Images / iStock: anouchka 26bl, Eloi_ Omella 32t, Eva-Katalin / E+ 27t, Gypsy Picture Show 54, Ingenui / E+ 135, Pgiam 6–7, 105t, Juergen Sack / E+ 128, saiko3p 25br, Starcevic 30, Xantana 73.

Holala Ibiza: 95.

La Mar Salada: 109.

Moments / Mandarin Oriental Hotel Group: George Apostolidis 117.

Dry Martini: Javier de las Muelas 115.

Nordic Think: 114b.

OMA Bistró Barcelona: 116.

Polaroids: 87.

Shutterstock.com: andysavchenko 71tl, Jana Asenbrennerova 97, csp 38t, Davix 129bl, Kirk Fisher 29br, Gimas 21cra, David Herraez Calzada 45, Jelena990 36cla, Mirages.nl 23b, Mitzo 40, NoyanYalcin 53tl, Berk Ozdemir 91t, Paulina Patalas-Krawczyk 12cr, Mounir Taha 17t, Sean Xu 17bl.

SuperStock: A. Burkatovski / Fine Art Images 31tl.

Tablao Flamenco Cordobes: 61.

Sheet Map Cover Image:
4Corners: Marco Arduino.

Cover Images:
Front and Spine: **4Corners:** Marco Arduino
Back: **Alamy Stock Photo:** Stefano Politi Markovina tr; **Dreamstime.com:** Boule13 tl, Noppasin Wongchum cl.

All other images © Dorling Kindersley Limited
For further information see: www.dkimages.com

Illustrator: Lee Redmond

A NOTE FROM DK

The rate at which the world is changing is constantly keeping the DK travel team on our toes. While we've worked hard to ensure that this edition of Barcelona is accurate and up-to-date, we know that opening hours alter, standards shift, prices fluctuate, places close and new ones pop up in their stead. So, if you notice we've got something wrong or left something out, we want to hear about it. Please get in touch at travelguides@dk.com

First edition 2002

Published in Great Britain by
Dorling Kindersley Limited,
DK, One Embassy Gardens, 8 Viaduct
Gardens, London SW11 7BW, UK

The authorised representative in the EEA is
Dorling Kindersley Verlag GmbH. Arnulfstr.
124, 80636 Munich, Germany

Published in the United States by
DK Publishing, 1745 Broadway, 20th Floor,
New York, NY 10019, USA

A CIP catalog record is available
from the British Library.

A catalog record for this book is available
from the Library of Congress.

ISSN: 1479-344X

ISBN: 978-0-2416-7566-3

Printed and bound in China

www.dk.com